# TRAVELS WITH A DAI

# Travels with a Dangerous Friend

Searching the world for a message in the bottle

## Anthony Fitzgerald

YOUCAXTON
PUBLICATIONS

Copyright © Anthony Fitzgerald 2024

The Author asserts the moral right to
be identified as the author of this work.

ISBN 978-1-915972-17-0 Published by YouCaxton Publications 2024

All rights reserved. No part of this publication may be reproduced, stored in a retrieval system, or transmitted in any form or by any means, electronic, mechanical, photocopying, recording or otherwise, without the prior permission of the author.

This book is sold subject to the condition that it shall not, by way of trade or otherwise, be lent, resold, hired out or otherwise circulated without the author's prior consent in any form of binding or cover other than that in which it is published and without a similar condition including this condition being imposed on the subsequent purchaser.

YouCaxton Publications
www.youcaxton.co.uk

To Tara, Petra, Pia, James and Mary Anne,
not forgetting Nicky and Judy who had to listen to all the stories,
but particularly with love to my very patient wife, Roseanne,
at whose instigation I wrote all this down.

# Chapter One

## CRASHING & BURNING

The psychiatrist was waving my form as he came back into the office where I was waiting expectantly.

'Usually, when we ask people to fill out these addiction questionnaires, we suggest to them that they've got a problem if three or four questions are ticked. You ticked sixteen'.

He conveyed this message in an almost congratulatory tone. As I'd got on rather well with him and had, what I'd thought, a rather amusing and intelligent conversation I smiled gratefully. But his next question threw me.

'Do you have medical insurance?'

I assured him that I had.

'In that case I strongly recommend that you check in here, as soon as possible, for a minimum of four weeks.'

Just a day or two later I was tucked up in an extremely comfortable room in The Priory at Marchwood. It was an elegant and sizeable Georgian house, set in beautiful well-treed grounds and with more than adequate food in the roomy and well laid out canteen. I did notice that some of my fellow diners looked a bit odd: A handful of emaciated girls with anorexia; an incredibly funny man of extraordinary verbal energy who turned out to be severely bi-polar; a bunch of rather depressed, watchful, generally middle-aged, men and women who turned out to be alcoholics; a gaggle of rebellious younger people, male and female, who were the drug addicts.

My first meeting was with the alcoholics. There were about seven or eight of us and I assumed I was with them for recreational purposes as I certainly wasn't an alcoholic. I drank socially. I drank quite a lot socially, but didn't everyone? My counsellor turned out to be a large, be-spectacled African American with a strong New York accent. He was not gentle; in fact he was pretty forceful, and it wasn't long before I found myself questioning some of his statements. That was a mistake.

'Are you some sorta Perfessor?' He asked with a grin eliciting some sniggering from the assembled alcoholics 'You're here to learn, not tell me what you think'.

It took around ten days for me to accept and admit to the group that I too, the grandiose Anthony Fitzgerald, was one of them. I was an alcoholic. My counsellor tore me apart and re-built me. It was an extraordinary process. The first morning started with the group of about eight of us, four men and four women, gathered in a circle with the counsellor, sitting in the circle. I was the new member of the group and had to introduce myself and explain why I thought I was there. Then it went round the circle with each person expanding on the stories of where their alcoholism had got them. I found myself genuinely interested in the stories but still felt like an onlooker. This was the usual format for the first ninety minutes each morning. The African American counsellor then lectured us, with the extensive use of a whiteboard, on various aspects of addiction. We discussed this with him and questioned his conclusions. I appeared initially to be at the forefront of the questioning until he skilfully de-constructed every question or interruption I put to him. I was not remotely ready to say the words 'I'm an alcoholic'.

I was never going to win this one. Over about ten days I reached a stage of submission which caused me to break down in tears on several occasions and to get incredibly angry on other occasions. My beliefs were questioned as well as my assumptions. The counsellor was himself an alcoholic and had been dry for twenty-five years. He had been counselling in the lower east side of Manhattan and had dealt with people far tougher and more intractable than us. Our group was predominantly middle-class, fairly rational and I suspect appeared to be much more acquiescent. There was one charming man looking not unlike a ravaged Peter O'Toole who escaped a couple of times down to the local pub. He left the course early and we learned later that he ended up in hospital in the last stages of liver failure. One particularly restful part of the treatment was to make us lie on our backs on the floor in a darkened room for an hour and a half with a variety of sounds, including the singing of whales and the crashing of waves, whilst colourful patterns were projected on to the ceiling. It didn't take that long to completely let go and fall asleep.

Towards the end of four weeks we were asked if we would like to ask our wives or husbands to take part in some sessions. My wife, Roseanne, was tracked down, and reluctantly agreed to take part. The counsellor who admitted to having been married six times, undoubtedly had problems of his own with women as well as alcohol and was extraordinarily brusque and domineering with Roseanne who walked out after the first of these sessions. I completely agreed with her on that occasion, but her very act of turning up was a breakthrough.

It took the entire four weeks, that the insurance company had agreed to pay for, to get to the stage where I could face the outside world and I started with three AA meetings a week to reinforce what I'd learned about myself.

After a while my wife saw that I was serious and returned. She offered me no great warmth but let it be known that if I was prepared to change, she would support me. For possibly the first time in my life, I came to realise how close I had come to crashing and burning and losing absolutely everything: My wife; my daughters; my house; my source of income and, as I was reminded, my life. I listened to the stories in AA meetings and heard how the crashes happened in real life to people just like me.

I had stopped just before closing time.

## TWENTY YEARS ON

Twenty years after my 'awakening' I walked through the woods near our house on a beautiful, if slightly misty, autumn morning in 2016. The temperature had cooled in the last few days, but it was still only a one-sweater walk. The ground was firm and dry. Leaves were dropping spasmodically from the trees. How can there be so many variations of yellow, gold, red and green?

I live happily with my tolerant and good-humoured wife and my ancient cat, in the woods of West Berkshire. I have just about stopped thinking of ways to earn money although, if a challenge appears, I'll probably go for it still. I'm healthy enough and not too unfit if a bit overweight. I have three daughters and a son all now in their thirties and forties. I get on well with all of them and may even be said to have crossed over from parent to friend. I am a lucky man by any measure.

So why do I want to write a book? I suppose at first glance it could be put down to self-aggrandisement or vanity, but on reading through the draft I cannot boast that there was a great deal to be vain about. I used to think it was because during the first ten years of my working life I earned my living as an advertising copywriter. I used to think too that I had a talent for writing and would one day be a successful novelist. Then there was the 'writing it for your children' motive. When I mentioned it to the youngest of my three daughters she groaned 'Daddy, we've heard all those stories a million times'. Not terribly encouraging really. I think it was in part because I wanted to bring back memories, to myself, of a time when you could get away with the things I got away with. As I started to write it became more obvious. I had to tell how I got from there to here. I had to write about how I nearly didn't make it.

I was never a dramatic drunk and most of my friends drank in a similar way. I didn't go around hitting people and I was always able to keep a job. I usually did not drink till after midday and on several occasions, I stopped completely for a week or two. I did however rely totally on alcohol to oil my wheels. In my mind it allowed me to get on better with people, to talk more freely, to be more creative, to be more exciting. Not to be boring. What an illusion that is. It also allowed me to fool everybody but my close family that I was totally in control of my life.

If I'm going to examine how I got into that way of life it is probably necessary to start at the beginning.

I was born to an Irish family. My father was an Irish-born British Army Officer in an Irish regiment. He came from a family with its roots in Cork. It was a reasonably well-off family as they were able to send him to a public school in England and later to Trinity

College, Dublin. It was also a family that lived at race-track speed. My grandfather's nickname was Monte Carlo Fitz. My father was the oldest of four siblings who were collectively known as the 'BlitzGeralds' in 1930's Dublin. As far as I can gather the two brothers and the two sisters all loved to party and were almost certainly all alcoholics. I'm pretty certain that this was to influence my later life. My mother had Anglo-Irish roots and her father had been a tea planter in Ceylon. She was considered a beauty and a good catch in Dublin society and my father was, as is told, a well-made man of great charm but, sadly with too many weaknesses, including an addiction to alcohol, for the marriage to survive.

My mother left him in 1946, a couple of years after my younger brother was born, when I was five, and made her way with us and our loyal Irish nanny to London. I was never to see him again.

In the forties in Britain it was a brave course of action for a woman from her background, in her mid-twenties, with two small sons, to strike out on her own and change countries. For two years she supported us. Her good looks enabled her to model for Pond's Face Cream and she worked in the offices of BOAC. Bearing in mind that she had done seasons in Vienna and Cairo and spoke good German and French this was not what she was expecting out of life. We lived in a flat above a Black and White Milk Bar, (you probably won't remember those unless you are in your seventies) in Kensington High Street. It was not the glamorous life for which she had been prepared, yet she managed to send me to the Gibbs School, then one of the smartest prep schools in London, where we paraded in crocodiles through the fashionable Kensington streets in our plum-coloured mob caps.

Happily, she had been furnished with good introductions and it was her good fortune, and ours, to attract the attention of Alan Muntz who was to become our stepfather. He was eighteen years older than she and it could probably be said that he remained deeply in love with her for the rest of his life.

Alan was a distinguished and engaging man. He had been a classical scholar at Winchester going on to get an engineering degree at Trinity College, Cambridge. Winchester's motto 'Manners maketh man' suited him entirely and he was always thoughtful and tolerant. We were so lucky that our mother found him. He had just taken part in the last few months of World War One as a young sapper officer and after the war joined, in Basra (present day Iraq), the Anglo-Iranian Oil Company, the precursor of BP I believe. A few years later he teamed up with Nigel Norman to found Airwork which had its origins in flying a biplane between Cairo, Alexandria and Benghazi. He was one of the founders of Heston Airport, of Middle East Airlines and aided J.R.D.Tata in the founding of Air India.

I remember that when he was courting my mother we used to be left, still in the company of our Irish nanny, in his palatial flat in Dorset Square which had the very latest radiogram and a collection of records. I got to know by heart, all the songs from 'South Pacific' in that flat.

A word about Nanny Bradbury. She was a very overweight Irish woman who could barely read or write but she was the most loyal, determined, dedicated and loving person. When my mother came over to England first, she wouldn't even take a wage as long as she had food and a roof over head. She saw it as her bounden duty to look after 'her boys' and my mother until life improved for us. I hasten to add that she was repaid when finally retired.

Alan moved us all to a beautiful house in Woburn Green, situated halfway between High Wycombe and Beaconsfield in Buckinghamshire. It was idyllic. A Queen Anne House set in eight acres with a lake and an island on it, the river Wye flowing through the grounds, an old water mill and a swimming pool. It was heaven for two small boys, and we revelled in it. Unfortunately, the upkeep was almost certainly too much for my stepfather to manage and my mother, realising that quickly, set about trying to make it all support itself. With her good friend Una Craddock, who took on the cottage on the estate, she set about creating an agri-business with deep litter pigs, mushroom growing and deep litter hens. It was back-breaking work for two women to undertake and it nearly destroyed my mother's health. It was around about then that she gave birth to my sister, Nicolette. My brother Jonathan and I remained oblivious to these pressures and adventured unheedingly in the wonderful playground it afforded us.

Alan with his customary benevolence undertook to send my brother and me to Gilling, the prep school for Ampleforth in Yorkshire. I was to spend a total of nine years in that beautiful valley in North Yorkshire being educated by the civilised and civilising Benedictine community. By and large I liked my time at school but there was one event that probably affected the rest of my life unfavourably.

When I was just thirteen the monk, who was headmaster of the house for boys between eleven and fourteen, made me Head of School and Captain of Rugby. It turned out to be more of a punishment than a privilege. I came across some activity that I can't even recall in detail but involved early sexual experimentation amongst a few of the other boys. As Head Boy, I told Father Peter about it and there were repercussions. In February, the playing fields were frozen solid and normal ball games were impossible. The whole school was therefore required to go on a run down to the brook in the valley, a distance of about two miles. In theory, the Head Boy was meant to be in charge of it but mostly it was just getting there and back without much opposition. That day was different. I felt the first stone hit me just before reaching the brook. I turned to find the whole school, some one hundred boys, facing me. Some of the boys I had reported then forced me into the brook, which was almost completely frozen and forced my head underwater. 'Let him up now!' One boy shouted, 'We might drown him'. I was allowed to regain the bank and, soaking wet in sub-zero temperatures, started the run back at the head of the school. I was crying openly. Apparently, apart from reporting the boys, which had triggered the incident, there was resentment at me being made Captain of Rugby over another of the boys who had been involved in leading the attack. As I sat in the refectory next to the headmaster still trying to hide my tears, the whole school was staring at me, to see if I was going to 'sneak' on them. I didn't. But I did carry the memory of that into the main school and for the rest of my school career. From then, I was very careful about shining too brightly. I was a good rugby player but even that was marred by several bone-breaks.

Looking back, I think, because of that incident, I became more frightened of total commitment. I had been, at prep school, in the scholarship stream but now rested in the form below and was no longer treated as a certain candidate for Oxbridge. I can't with honesty say that my life was totally blighted by this, but I am certain it did affect my confidence, exacerbate my shyness and make me feel more isolated.

Leaving Ampleforth, which otherwise passed without major incident, saw me back with my parents, having obtained only moderate academic qualifications, but otherwise prepared to take on adult life and with every intention of going to work and building a career, at the start of one of the most exciting decades of a lifetime.

I now look back on the sixties which were to come as a decade full of hope, opportunity and fun. Let's face it the predictable, grey, rationed fifties of my teenage years had to be an improvement, although I was protected from most of the downside, I was able to play a part in a decade of colour, creativity and innocent hedonism. It was the decade when the birth control pill arrived, and women reacted accordingly. It was the era of The Beatles, of Carnaby Street and the King's Road. You could travel the world without much let or hindrance on a British passport and you could get employment of some sort or other almost anywhere.

I loved my middle-class parents but in hindsight they were a strange in-between generation. Born almost in the Edwardian era they felt strongly that having good manners was the ultimate accolade, behaving like a gentleman, with expectations achieved by the judicious use of social and business contacts. You did not stray from your pre-destined path.

In the war that generation evolved collectively into quiet heroes. Well-starched upper lips were in evidence everywhere. They suffered and were remarkable and brave. After the war they 'got on with it' in a bruised, battered and impoverished Britain and lived through the boring early fifties with equanimity, regarding those years almost as an extension of the war. The sixties could be said to have burst upon them, and they were thrust into a glittering and, to them, a totally irrepressible age. Anyone who's seen The Wizard of Oz will remember black and white Kansas and technicolour Oz. Their children, now in their teens and early twenties, were a different species, hardly recognisable. It was as though one and a half, or even two generations, rather than a single generation, separated us from our parents. It was difficult for both of us, and the changing values created conflict that impelled many of the young, including me, to make a break for a totally undefined freedom, wherever it lay.

# Chapter Two

## YOUNG MAN GOING WEST

As with most comfortably brought-up middle-class youths leaving school at that time, I had no inkling of the meandering route my life would take. Leaving school at eighteen in 1959 with no idea about the future, my parents made it clear, lovingly but firmly, that I had to earn a living straight away. I hadn't met the earlier expectations of getting into Trinity College, Cambridge, which had been my stepfather's old college.

My American uncle, Don Kennedy, married to my mother's younger sister Barbara, and a colonel in the US Marines, was a large and cheerful man with the American equivalent of a military moustache and extraordinarily bright blue eyes. He had all the openness of a man born and brought up in the western states, in his case, Montana. He had been one of the very youngest US Marine colonels in the war when he had met Barbara. He and Barbara, who had assimilated the trait, common to most Americans, of positive optimism, were generous and loved partying. Don, who was then dividing his time between Paris and London as something to do with S.H.A.P.E., the headquarters of NATO, offered to try and get me into advertising. He introduced me to one of his drinking companions, Tom Reynolds, the American managing director of Young & Rubicam in London. I remember turning up and announcing that I wanted to write. Tom was friendly but nonplussed.

'Let's get this straight. You're eighteen and have been at a boarding school for the last ten years. Don't you think you might need some life experience to actually write about? Why not travel for a year or two and then come back and see me?'

I almost heard his sigh of relief as I left his office, his duty to my uncle discharged.

I was used to doing as I was told so that very same day saw me down at the US Embassy in Grosvenor Square to obtain the forms for emigrating to the USA. With the help of Uncle Don, I was on an immigrant flight within weeks, with one hundred dollars in my pocket, a gift from my puzzled stepfather who had assumed I would go to Cambridge.

I was to fly in a turbo prop Britannia from one of the less fashionable airports. I think Northolt. It stopped like some great flying bus at Manchester, Glasgow and Boston before disgorging me in New York. It took something like twenty hours, but I did get to see the Northern Lights from my window seat. It is hard to do them justice in words because they were so unexpectedly huge. They seemed to spread out from one end of the horizon to the other and the colours, every shade of blue, green and yellow, ever-changing, were unlike anything I could have expected to see.

I knew enough about saving money to check into the YMCA in West 34th St. I was a tall, skinny blond youth, innocent and naive. Within hours a kindly Scotsman, whom I should have recognised as unmistakably gay, engaged me in conversation. I knew little about homosexuals nor how to recognise them. He was kind enough to realise that I wasn't one of his persuasion.

'You really shouldn't be staying here you know' he said, and he explained why.

I ended up in a bedsit in the distinctly unfashionable Lower East Side. The first few days I spent in Times Square cinemas rejoicing in my wealth and freedom. Meals were from coin-in-the-slot places like Horn & Hardart. What a life I was leading!

By the end of my first week in New York there was no money left.

I rang my one really impressive contact, Gordon Selfridge, a senior Vice President at Sears Roebuck, the son of the man who had come over to England from America in 1909 to found the eponymous department store. He, despite his American antecedents, had been schooled at Winchester and was a friend and contemporary of my stepfather Alan. He was a tall, reserved man who was not displaying a great sense of humour.

'I was kind of expecting you to call' he said. 'Get a bus over to the West Side and come see me.'

'Actually, this call has just taken my last ten cents.'

There was a moment's silence, then,

'you'd better walk, it will take you about forty minutes.'

The elegant English secretary, standard issue for the top echelons of American business in late 1959, led me into a palatial corner office in the mighty Sears Roebuck Building.

He didn't waste time.

'Sue, come here and witness an IOU.'

Turning to me he said

'I'm going to lend you ten dollars. If you haven't got a job within twenty-four hours, I'll buy you

an air ticket back to London. I don't suppose you'll feel too great about that?'

I signed the IOU witnessed by the secretary who was desperately trying to stop laughing. It took me a good thirty minutes to overcome the humiliation, but I bought a copy of the Daily News and settled down to read the jobs section.

Hot from an English boarding school education I don't suppose anybody at home thought that I should be working in a pink apron down at D'Agostino's Supermarket on East 25$^{th}$ and 3$^{rd}$ Ave in Manhattan. There were a lot of strange looks, double takes and intrusive questions when I worked the tills in this shabby neighbourhood with my supposedly posh English accent. But it was a job and it paid fifty-five dollars a week. It was around the corner from my cheap bedsit, and it covered rent and food.

The next move was to inveigle myself into an ad agency. The Young & Rubicam Managing Director in London had given me the name of a Senior Vice President at Young & Rubicam in New York and I made contact. He agreed to see me and then suggested lunch with a colleague. I found myself with two friendly and mildly amused senior men who, decades later, both attained the position of Chairman of Young & Rubicam. One was Bill Colihan, and the other was Steve

Frankfurt. They were relaxed, charming and exuded success and, in inviting me to lunch, it was obvious that they didn't have much on that day. They suggested dry martinis. I had never had a dry martini before but accepted. Within twenty minutes I was over-talkative, supremely confident and sharing my views on most things. Clearly, I was drunk. I think they found it hilarious. Hilarious enough to suggest I come and work in the mail room at Y&R. I had just taken the fabled first step onto a Madison Avenue career in early 1960.

Directed to the basement of 285 Madison Avenue, I found myself working a mimeograph machine in the company of several others of approximately my age including a blindingly crude young Sicilian and a Turk newly arrived in the States, who was friendly and charming. We delivered the results of our copying machines around the building to all the beautiful people who had proper jobs and decent suits. I had never seen women like that. In the heyday of Marilyn Monroe, it was the era of exaggerated curvature. I had yearning eyes for them, but they certainly did not have eyes for me. They were zeroing in on the young Account Executives and Directors, hot from Yale, Harvard and Princeton. They were looking at a comfortable life, two and a half children, with a house in Westchester or Greenwich beckoning. I just delivered the copies, and I was still only getting fifty-five dollars a week. The television series 'Madmen', made fifty years later, was no exaggeration.

I desperately needed to earn more money. In those days one could get fifteen dollars for donating a pint of blood every six weeks, so that was a start. Then I saw an ad for contestants in a television quiz show. To my considerable surprise they selected me for a CBS nation-wide show, and I was one of three contestants who had to pitch a story about my alleged family crest. I was given the Schaeffer's Ice Cream crest; the second contestant was I think given the Marlborough Cigarette crest and the third highly unlikely American talked about his own family crest. I was the only English person. I didn't convince the audience and was given a hundred dollars for taking part, but the real bonus was that Brenda Lee, the Southern bombshell of a singer, then aged about sixteen, was also on the show and her presence gave me something to think about for weeks after and to swoon over 'Sweet Nothings'. I still do.

Another source of income meant giving up my Saturdays in the rapidly over-heating New York summer to join a carload of other young men who were also looking for extra income, and we were all taken to Bedford Stuyvesant, the predominantly African American area of the huge New York suburb of Queens and dropped off at intervals. We were each assigned a tenement block and all day we would knock on doors to enquire about cockroaches.

'Excuse me, Ma'am, are you troubled by cockroaches?'

'Sure, we got roaches. Where you from white boy?'

questioned the massively overweight Afro American lady.

This got the conversation going and I would be admitted with my two gallon can and spray gun, ignoring the curious looks of the Harlem Globetrotter sized men lounging about in the apartment. As was usual the walls were crawling with cockroaches. The technique was to fix on a really big one and drown and poison it in one efficient squirt. It always got a sale, because in those bigoted days it was assumed that white people always knew what was best for black people, and I used to double my weekly wage in one day, but it was hot work particularly as I always wore a suit because I'd always understood that was the correct code of dress for a 'professional'.

The overriding recollection was that all the black folk were inevitably friendly and patient. It was 1960 however and the Black Power movement, which didn't really take off as a particularly violent movement until 1966, when led by Stokely Carmichael and later Malcolm X, was just in its infancy. I do remember walking through the slum in ninety-five-degree heat and humidity, absolutely exhausted at the end of the day and being hailed from a deserted building site by two large black ladies. They were barbecuing something that smelled delicious. 'Hey, white boy, you like spareribs?' I was treated to a couple of ribs and a cold beer. They had realised that I had been working all day and I suppose had just taken pity. It was one of my best and most enduring memories of America.

I had ended up sharing a two-room apartment in a six-storey building in Brooklyn Heights, then a slightly run-down but rising suburb just over the East River in the shadow of the Brooklyn Bridge. I mention that it was six storeys because we had the corner apartment on the sixth floor with a flat roof, in a New York summer, with permanent ninety-degree heat and humidity, and no air conditioning. We used to take it in turns on some nights to lie for hours in the bath full of cold water. My English flatmate was the rather entitled scion of a major ship-broking company. He was doing a year's stint to gain experience in the New York office as a twenty-three-year-old, so basically four years older. He behaved as though he was twenty years older, and he earned, I calculated, around four times what I was being paid by Y&R. However, he absolutely insisted on every little thing being split down the middle. No quarter given!

It wasn't all work though. In those days I really loved trad jazz and was a great fan of Louis Armstrong. I managed to get a ticket for a jazz concert at Madison Square Gardens where the line-up was, impossibly, Louis Armstrong, Dizzy Gillespie, Count Basie, Gene Krupa, the Modern Jazz Quartet, Ahmad Jamal, Sarah Vaughan, Woody Herman and many other greats. The ticket, then was just one dollar fifty and it was right up in the 'bleachers' in the company of several thousand African Americans all high on pot which was something else I knew nothing about. But what a concert! I was later to go to very nearly the same line-up in an outdoor concert in the Columbia Stadium on a hot summer's night.

The English secretary of my Sears Roebuck contact had been told to keep an eye on me and she sent my way a couple of invitations to cocktail parties revolving around junior diplomats at the UN and the British Consulate. At one party, I listened fascinated to the tales of a daring young Englishman from his recent experiences as a mercenary for Baptista in Cuba, the leader who was of course overthrown by the long-lived Fidel Castro. These parties provided quite a contrast to my otherwise rather humdrum existence but as a rather shy nineteen-year-old I didn't exactly make an impression.

Until I met the divine Carol.

Across the room at one of these parties I caught the eye of a really attractive girl. She was slim, very pretty and fashionably dressed. She smiled, and I think I made my way across to her but maybe it was the other way around.

She asked, if I remember rightly,

'Are you planning to eat somewhere?"

I feigned a reaction that showed clearly that I was used to getting questions like that from girls like her.

'Yes, are you? Maybe we could find somewhere...?'

It really was a coup de foudre. She led me to a restaurant somewhere in the fashionable East Sixties where a whole week's wages went on wining and dining this gorgeous girl who appeared to be interested in what I had to say. I was smitten, and we spent hours and days together in that hot summer, wandering around New York art galleries and museums, or in her smart East Side apartment.

I remember too going with Carol to a night club near Times Square where Louis Armstrong was playing. They must have liked the look of us because we were given a table right next to the stage, a couple of feet away from the great man. Rather embarrassingly I couldn't order any alcohol because I was under twenty-one and it was against the law in New York State. I had to order orange juice for us both. The experience was way beyond my means because I recklessly paid the cover price for a second session, but it was worth every penny to hear my idol up close.

Carol had told me that she'd been engaged to a young US Army officer who had been killed in Korea. The very bloody Korean War, which America and Britain entered in 1950, when the communist North aided by the Chinese invaded the South, had ended back in 1953. I suppose I should have 'done the math'. I was so naïve that it came as a real shock when she disclosed over the months that followed that she was thirty-five, sixteen years older than I. She certainly didn't look it, but my overreaction was ridiculously immature and the whole thing ended I suppose because I felt that I'd been misled. It was a mistake I regretted for a long time.

Back at Young & Rubicam I was called in by Personnel and told of a Market Research job in Chicago, for which I might be suited. I leapt at it.

'Yes, please. How do I get there?'

This was America.

'We don't know. Just get there.'

It was to take around twenty-two hours on a Greyhound Bus, and cost me a week's wages. No travel allowance then. We were in the socially mobile society. I had to borrow $30 from my stuffy English flatmate. He was disparaging as usual but grudgingly lent me the thirty bucks.

I set off at the weekend, overnight on the bus, and twenty-four hours later made my way to the YMCA in downtown Chicago. I knew how to handle 'Ys' now. The next morning I reported to Young and Rubicam on Michigan Boulevard. It was early October 1960 and John F. Kennedy had been elected the Democratic Presidential candidate in July and was to become President in November. Mayor Richard Daley was well into his long and sometimes controversial rule as Mayor of Chicago. It was also the beginning of October, and I really wasn't prepared for the full impact of the Chicago winter to come.

My new boss, Dick Frost, a smallish man of around twenty-five who dressed in a conventionally 'preppy' way and wore glasses, had recently got his doctorate at the University of Chicago which would have made him very bright indeed. Dick was pleasant enough to me and got me started in market research. After a week or so he suggested that he was looking for someone to share an apartment and I jumped at the opportunity. Now I didn't know much about the right suburb to live in, but I would never have picked the South Side of Chicago. That's where we ended up. He had an attachment to the area, having studied at the nearby University of Chicago. The South Side contained one of the largest black urban populations in America. It was still a period when, just two years later in 1962, that President Kennedy dispatched troops to force the University of Mississippi to admit James Meredith, a black student. At the same time, he forbade racial or religious discrimination in federally financed housing.

Although back in 1960 the first rumblings of racial tension were only being faintly heard, and the boot was very firmly on the white foot, it still made me slightly uneasy walking the mile from the nearest 'L' Station on 51$^{st}$ St. It also made me bloody cold as the temperature and the wind brought it down on occasions to minus twenty degrees. There's a song by the famous Chicago born singer Lou Rawls where he describes the wind, roaring off Lake Michigan from Canada to the north, as 'The Almighty Hawk'. They had to put ropes up on the sidewalk outside our Michigan Boulevard office to stop people being blown into the road.

The first night in our new apartment, on the second floor of a house belonging to a Rabbi and his wife, friends of Dick's, was a bit of a revelation. We had a room each and a few minutes after I had turned in, the door opened, and Dick sat down on my bed, reaching out a hand to stroke my leg. I leapt up in horror.

'What the hell are you doing?' I squealed.

That's when Dick started laughing.

'Oh God, I'm sorry. I kind of thought you must be one of us, being English and all that.'

It all resolved itself amicably and Dick said I was free to find somewhere else, but he wouldn't mind me staying as long as he could bring guys back and I could bring girls back. The chances of that were highly unlikely as I didn't actually know anyone and was still pretty awkward. However, he was so friendly about it that I agreed. That began a good friendship and a lot of extraordinary encounters over the next six months.

There was the party in our house, predominantly gay (a term not used in 1960) at which were half the professors at the University of Chicago where one Bevode McCall, an eminent sociologist who I believe worked with the famous Vance Packard (of 'Hidden Persuaders' fame), charged amorously at one young man and took the entire wooden balustrade into the garden below. It was like a scene from an old Western.

Then there was the little party Dick gave for the, mostly male, members of the touring Royal Ballet. There were some famous names there, but I can't now recall them. It was a touch incongruous down in the South Side of Chicago.

Dick was a Bridge Master and champion of the Mid-West. I recall one extraordinary evening when I was asked to make up a Bridge Foursome on our humble kitchen table, to enable them to practice for a major tournament, with the Bridge champion of the Far West and Adam Meredith the British World Champion at the time. I basically had to just sit there and do as I was told while they rehearsed moves. The scene was quite surreal.

It was in Chicago that I had my first experience of drugs. I had met a lot of strange people in Chicago but one of the strangest was an itinerant hippy who was on the edge of our group of friends. He was a nice enough guy but definitely not part of the corporate world. He disappeared for a few weeks after I first met him but surfaced again, having come up from New Mexico by bus, at a friend's house where we were sitting around having a few beers. He had what looked like a carry-on airline bag slung over his shoulder and he tipped it out on the floor. All it contained were peyote roots the size of small turnips. Peyote roots I've always understood are the raw material for mescaline which is another word for LSD. We cooked up a few roots and I was persuaded to eat one. The world very quickly became much more colourful, the music playing was exquisite, and the conversation was brilliant. Everything was enhanced. About an hour into the experience, I think, I rushed from the room and was violently ill. I never touched it again.

Dick invited me to accompany him for the long Thanksgiving weekend with his family in Minneapolis. It was at least a nine-hour train journey and I remember the largest meal I have ever eaten. We appear to have been given a whole turkey each by his largely Scandinavian-American family. The train journey back was a drunken riot with the entire carriage joining in poker games.

Then the office organized a trip over the New Year holiday to go skiing in Boyne Falls, Michigan. We went by bus, but the three days skiing turned into two as we were marooned by a huge snowstorm for a whole day in a diner in Kalamazoo. When we got to Boyne the skiing was on a very small hill indeed and as Boyne Falls was right up on the Canadian border it was unbelievably cold.

Thanks to the entertainment value of the largely gay circles I moved in, I really loved my time in Chicago. It's a great city with fantastic energy and no pretensions. Whilst everybody in New York kept saying to any passing Englishman 'say it again. You say it so beautifully' I can't recall any Chicagoan ever even commenting on the fact that I talked 'funny'. Also, one of the benefits of being the only straight guy in a circle of gay people was that the women who hung around with gays, the 'fags molls', invariably found a need for sex. It wasn't all bad.

My uncle Don, now in charge of the US Marine recruiting programme at Parris Island, South Carolina, was insistent that I should come down and stay so that he could check up on me and, as it turned out, attempt to recruit me. Parris Island was, alarmingly, rather well known for the Ribbon Creek incident in 1956, when Staff Sergeant Matthew McKeon, a junior drill instructor, marched his platoon into a swampy tidal creek. The incident resulted in the deaths of six US Marine Corps recruits and was often held up as an example of the rigidity of US Marine training.

So, eager to get to this sub-tropical haven in the South, I set off again diagonally across America with the Greyhound Bus line. This took over twenty-four hours. On the way, for the last couple of hundred miles, we started to pick up an assortment of young men. Most of them were unprepossessing and most were attempting to fashion themselves on Elvis Presley, who by then was just about to leave the US Army after a two-year stint. I went back to sleep.

I was awakened by a huge black Marine Sergeant standing in the bus doorway screaming at us all. The assembled Elvis's all scrambled out, me amongst them, and were told to line up, stop talking and take our clothes off. I eventually persuaded one of the two genuinely frightening Sergeants that I was a visitor and not a recruit. My fellow travellers were then led off, stripped buff naked and had all their hair shaved off, including their Elvis quiffs.

The three weeks spent with my uncle were curious. He was determined to make an American, and therefore a man, of me. He was confident that I would make a magnificent Marine in time and that my parents back in England would welcome the improvement. I just knew they wouldn't. I did take part in the assault course and, as I had only recently finished nine years at an English boarding school on the Yorkshire Moors playing rugby, I was as fit as any of the raw recruits. I did get a sight of some of the recruits who had completed six months training though, and they were totally unrecognizable. I was certainly not at their level then. Don attempted to show me how nirvana could be attained by playing golf with me on the officers' golf course in the afternoons, but I wasn't convinced. I had to get out of there.

It wasn't far this time. Just seventy-five miles up the coast to the beautiful town of Charleston South Carolina, a lot of whose inhabitants didn't seem to acknowledge that there had been a Civil War around a century earlier, let alone that they might have lost it. I found lodgings down on The Battery, near the waterfront, with two dear ante-bellum ladies. The street was charming, and all the houses were painted in pastel colours. It couldn't have been more elegant, more peaceful or more unlike the America of Parris Island.

My way of trying to earn a living here was to enrol as a World Book encyclopaedia salesman. I was trained by a formidable lady in her fifties who would not have been out of place in the shires of England. It was a ruthless technique. You located a 'poor white' household and if the door was opened by a young white mother it went like this.

'Are you worried about your children's education?'

'Sure am.'

'Do you think the State does enough to help with your children's education?'

'Sure don't.'

At this stage you hit them with the plan. Pay ten dollars a month for two years and you could have all the knowledge in the world to share with your treasured children.

The closest I got to a sale was to a young mother, hardly older than I, already with three children and visibly impoverished. She was all set to sign up when something inside me said, "No", and I walked away. My lady boss was contemptuous and dismissive. That was the end of that scam.

Before I left Charleston, I was taken by my two charming landladies to a meeting of the English-Speaking Union. Charleston, after Boston, was one of the strongholds of the ESU. They seemed to still fancy that England was going to allow them to ship their cotton out to the mills of Manchester as happened in 1850, pre-bellum. A certain class of Charlestonian, white, genteel and elderly, just loved the British and the Civil War was referred to as the 'recent troubles.

We arrived at the ESU, the two ladies on my arm making me feel like Clark Gable in 'Gone with the Wind'. Fans a flutter and teacups poised we sat through a volatile talk from the Dame of Sark, Sybil Hathaway. She spared us nothing as she related the horrors of the German occupation in the early 1940's. She talked of rape and pillage, and she was very good at bringing it to life. At the end of her talk I was wheeled forward as the only other English person in the room. Dame Sybil talked affably to me, but what I really remember, when nobody was looking, was the fat wink that she gave me, as much as to say that she knew we were both trading on our nationality and she wouldn't tell if I wouldn't.

As a failed encyclopaedia salesman, I headed back to the familiar embrace of Young and Rubicam in New York. Rather surprisingly they took me back as a Market Research junior executive. It was at this time that I met a couple of English girls who were travelling around, and we had a memorable long weekend down in Williamsburg, which had been the capital of Virginia in the eighteenth Century until just after Independence, and Jamestown the first permanent English settlement in 1607. Some people say that's where the British Empire began. The place was full of kindly people dressed in authentic eighteenth-century clothes telling you to have a good day in twentieth century American accents.

It was a much easier stay in New York this time and I was settling in nicely when my life was rudely interrupted in mid-1961 by a notice from the US draft board to present myself for call-up. This I had not planned for and mercifully my sympathetic stepfather gave me the money for a ticket back to England. It was just as well, as full USA involvement in the Vietnam War was to be in 1965. For all I know I could still be on the run from the US Army fifty-five years later.

Looking back on my time in the States so long ago, I cannot say that alcoholic drink came into my American existence. I was endlessly thinking on my feet about surviving financially. It now seems extraordinary, given what happened later in my life, that I had the confidence to do what I did. I was unbelievably naïve, and probably took risks where I never even started to imagine the consequences.

Back in England I did not stay at home with my parents for very long. Looking back I realize that the USA had unsettled me. I had seen real life, earned my own living and somehow survived. I irritated a lot of people, but I suspect mainly my family, by adopting American ways and talking endlessly about all the good points of the USA. I never brought up the bad side. They were glad when I went up to London and walked into Y&R's offices again.

The American Managing Director who sent me off unwittingly was still there.

He was surprised to see me.

'Do you mean you actually went abroad as I suggested?'

'Yes. And I worked for Young & Rubicam in New York and Chicago.'

He was so astonished at me pulling this off that he offered me a graduate training position starting in Marketing. I fixed up a bedsit share in Knightsbridge with another Y&R trainee and was determined to be a success.

Britain, after the heady years under 'You've never had it so good' Harold Macmillan and then the brief reign of Lord Home, was shortly to lurch to the left under Harold Wilson. Everything was still rather cushy for the middle and upper classes. The working-class population was definitely beginning to realise that they had just as much right to the prosperity. We danced to The Beatles, the Rolling Stones, Elvis Presley, Gerry and the Pacemakers and Herman's Hermits. Our girlfriends shopped at Mary Quant and Biba in Kensington Church Street. We went to the 'flics' and lapped up the early Bond films and the 'spaghetti westerns. Television consisted of just two channels. When on the move you phoned from a red phone box or the phone in the pub. Everybody went to the pub.

For me though London proved a lot lonelier than I had thought it would be. The confidence I felt in America rather evaporated because I no longer stood out as an Englishman in a foreign country. In America I wasn't required to do much more than be an Englishman. To my mind it made me exceptional without having to show the real me, which I hadn't yet identified. It enabled me to hide my vulnerability. In my own country I was expected to knuckle down and rely on my own hard work and personality. It was the first time that I was thus challenged. My few school friends had moved on in the two years I'd been away, so I repaired to the nearest public house, The Bunch of Grapes in Knightsbridge, sometimes referred to as the Vatican Arms or the Crossed Keys due to its proximity to the Oratory, the well-known Catholic church.

The Bunch of Grapes became home for the first few months. I loved the louche atmosphere. Smoke-filled and dimly lit with red velvet and dark wood everywhere, it was filled too with half the eccentrics in London. I spent hours drinking with 'the last tinker in Knightsbridge', also with the infamous Roberta Cowell, she/he of indeterminate gender, and an assortment of public schoolboy dropouts. It was good fun, but it certainly gave momentum to what became a nearly life-long reliance on alcohol. It gave me confidence and allowed me to be admitted to the groups that I thought had wit and wisdom which, in hindsight, was an awfully long way from the truth. I think this was probably where the first seeds of addiction were sown.

The job and the pay in my new job were more than satisfactory. It was a fabulous opportunity to advance myself, but London grew more alluring. I then graduated to living in a house off the King's Road belonging to 'Sam' Anstis, the girl I had met in New York and with whom we'd driven down to Williamsburg. That moved me into Chelsea which I felt to be, for no particularly good reason, my natural habitat.

The King's Road had such a great atmosphere compared to the rest of London. The prettiest girls in the newly arrived mini dresses paraded up and down, attracted by the original and quirky shops. I had a red mini and parked up on the pavement every night at The

Clarence or The Denmark or 'The Duke of Boots' or The Australian. To my mind I now had a thousand friends. The trouble with that was that they were all in the pubs. It was a lot of fun, but it was a dangerous road. I'm certain that was when I started to need alcohol to bolster my self-confidence and to overcome shyness. The illusion that you might be considered entertaining after a couple of drinks. The feeling of camaraderie when with others drinking at the same place and speed was also illusory but of course I couldn't begin to realise it at that stage in my life.

The big fall came in the shape of a drunken escapade with two friends, one a girl called Buzz I recollect and the other, Jeremy, with whom I had been at school. We drove all round Putney and Hammersmith drunkenly trying to find unlocked cars from which we were going to get rich. Our haul was I think three road atlases and an old mac. The policeman who pulled us over was disbelieving at our stupidity as we were patently drunk. Back then drink driving didn't seem to matter and we were hauled in front of the magistrate's court on the next morning in Putney and thankfully merely told to go away and behave ourselves. Unfortunately, it was a day light on big news, and we had a small mention in the Evening Standard Londoner's Diary mainly caused by Jeremy telling the policeman that he was related to the Duke of Edinburgh. Needless to say, Jeremy wasn't related to anyone of any significance, but this arrogance annoyed the policeman so much that he rang the newspaper.

I was humiliated beyond belief and went in to Young and Rubicam and tendered my resignation.

'You don't have to do that' said my boss 'We think you're an idiot, but we recognize the difference between drunken behaviour and criminality. You'd be a better person by facing up to the embarrassment.'

To my shame I just couldn't be that 'better person'. At that stage an older trainee colleague, Dettmar Hackman, took me for a drink and introduced me to the next chapter of my erratic life.

# Chapter Three

## THE BUMPY ROAD TO AUSTRALIA

At this stage in my life, I was probably feeling more bewildered than anything else. Everything had happened so quickly, emanating from one drunken escapade to an evening spent talking to a bunch of strangers in a pub about driving to Australia.

I was introduced to a group of engineers who had worked together at International Harvester, including an Australian who wanted to go home and an ex-German private soldier and POW who had stayed on in England after the war, plus two cousins and one girl. They were going to drive to Melbourne, Australia and they needed a couple more bodies to spread the cost.

The first meeting was in the Ladbroke Arms in Notting Hill Gate and the others viewed me with dismay. Whilst they were not exactly in overalls most of them looked as though they had got into their gardening clothes and then spent the afternoon stripping their cars down. I had moved from wanting to be Oscar Wilde to my Burlington Bertie phase. Pin-striped, white collar over Bengal stripes, a furled umbrella. Trying to give the impression of immeasurable wealth and breeding. I was more than a bit insecure in those days. They came from a real world of work and of making things. I came from the world of talking and writing about things. We were miles apart.

They questioned me closely. 'You know that we'll spend about three months driving through inhospitable country mostly with bugger all roads?' 'You realize we'll all be in one tent?' The subtext was 'you look like a drip and won't be any use to us at all!' Things brightened up slightly when I told them that I had spent nearly two years bumming round the States. Grudgingly they accepted me.

In fact, there were about six hundred applications to join them, of which around sixty could be regarded as serious. You may wonder about this response, but it is worth pointing out that an expedition of this length and duration was a rare event in the early sixties. They were hoping to attract a doctor to the group, and another girl to keep the single girl company. I scored points by producing my friend and landlady, Sam. She was a formidable person, nearly six feet tall with a mass of bright red hair and a keen intelligence and wit. On reflection it may well be the reason that my application to join them survived.

There followed, over several weeks, a tedious series of organisational meetings. Back in 1962 we were only aware of three sizeable expeditions that had driven from London to Singapore. One was Princess Margaret's boyfriend, Group Captain Peter Townsend with unlimited funds and certainly countless introductions and diplomatic clearances. The Oxford & Cambridge expedition was in 1956, I think. The third was the British Army. In the years following our expedition many people made the journey and it became known as the 'Hippy Trail' for those who dropped out in Nepal. In 1962 it had not been undertaken mainly because of the lack of roads. Afghanistan had none then and much of Turkey and Iran consisted of pot-holed and corrugated dirt roads. Yugoslavia was still determinedly communist and not noticeably cooperative.

Then there was the problem of visas for just about every country. They took weeks to get and a lot of persistence. There were certainly physical and medical hazards which to be overcome, as we found out at our cost. The only way we could communicate was by way of 'poste restantes' at the main post offices in major towns and picking up three-week-old letters. I'm sure you are aware that mobile telephones and computers had not yet been invented, and I do not recall even making a phone call during the four months that we eventually took.

Our 'early adopter' status allowed us to beg for help and over several weeks more than twelve hundred letters were sent out to embassies, travel bureaus and, importantly, companies who might be willing to sponsor us. We were given a lot of supplies from companies, notably Johnson and Johnson, Bayer, Firestone and, incongruously, Wrigley's Chewing Gum.

Two short wheel-based Series 1 Land Rovers of 1953 and 1956 vintage were bought from a bankrupt Norfolk farmer for one hundred and eighty pounds (around £4,700 in today's money). The price gives an indication as to their condition. The two litre petrol engines gave a top speed of not much more than fifty miles per hour. They came with two doors and a canvas roof. Rik and Jim, a qualified mechanic, spent two months re-building them. We painted them, for some reason a bright, pale blue, and painstakingly drew a map of our route, together with a list of our suppliers, on the side. To the two Land Rovers was added a two-wheel trailer which had to carry the heavy canvas army surplus tent designed for eight soldiers and in which ten of us slept each night.

As four months were to be spent in such close company, I need to introduce the cast. Our leader was Angus 'Gus' Gibb (24 years old), muscular and bespectacled, ex-National Service with the Ghurkas and an energetic and empathetic leader. The other founding member was Larry Ford (24), a laid –back Australian looking for an original way to get home. Tim Groome (23), ex-navy National Service with a bent for efficiency bordering on the insane, Alan Stewart (22) was a well-balanced chap who occasionally wore clothes that did not look as though they had come from a charity. Rik Banham (24) was Gus's rather bombastic cousin. Pat Culshaw was Tim's cousin, distinguished by a full beard that he grew in about two and a half days. I have to say that Pat's personality did not have much effect on me, and I cannot recall much about him. Then there was the essential Josef 'Jim' Stich (39) an ex-German prisoner of war, who had been so ashamed of Germany after the war that he had stayed on. He had been working as a bartender at the local Suffolk pub where they all first met and, mercifully, he was a brilliant mechanic. The first girl in was Maggie Rought-Rought (which really was her surname), 19, the daughter of a Norfolk landowner, another Amazon of nearly six feet tall with a mane of blond hair and a permanent smile. Val 'Sam' Anstis I have already described. Finally, there was me, aged twenty-one, and considered a liability by the oil-covered others.

I have wondered often about my relationship with the Overlanders, as we grandly referred to ourselves. I knew nothing of their world of engineering and practicality. I felt a bit useless when it came to replacing a fan belt or a spark plug. I did feel that I knew more about the countries we would be going through and was certainly more curious than they were. They just wanted to get to Australia and have an adventure. I did feel on the periphery, and I found it hard to impress my views on the group. It was a feeling that I was becoming used to. It was a feeling that later in life led to me seeking the false confidence of a few stiff drinks. I never felt able to take the lead because I hadn't really developed any self-awareness, as I'd not needed to identify my real personality in the States. I was destined apparently to be just a crew member.

Eccentrically for an overland trip, the first leg was by plane on the 30$^{th \, of}$ August 1962 from Lydd Airport for Le Touquet in a transporter that took the two Land Rovers and the trailer with the army surplus tent. It was expedient because the plane fitted our load and our team exactly, so it cost less than a ferry.

In France almost immediately I drove a Frenchman off the road. It was all sorted out in the spirit of entente cordiale, and we proceeded to Belgium where we insisted on getting our passports stamped, to the noticeable irritation of the Belgian gendarmerie. The reasoning was that our sponsors might need proof of where we had been.

In one small village Mags, Sam and I went foraging in the villagers' vegetable plots. Not good behaviour, looking back on it, but we were determined not to get scurvy or indeed to spend any unnecessary money on food. Ashamedly, it was not the last time we went foraging in this manner.

We picked up Larry in Munich. He had been touring around with his girlfriend (later his wife) Judy. Everything was unpacked all over the Munich Northwest Camp site and we went to find the Hofbräuhaus. Larry was every inch an Ozzie. He was lean, fit, and thin-lipped, a peculiar characteristic of Australians that I seem to have noticed. He was humorous and thoughtful with a sardonic wit. On the entire trip I never saw him in anything but a tee shirt, truly short shorts, and flip-flops. An alien from outer space would have immediately seen that he was different from the rest of us, in the nicest possible way.

The next day Larry went exploring and came back with a small, humourless-looking man who misled us by turning out to be good-humoured to the point of lunacy. He announced that he would be paying for our camp site and proceeded to donate cigarettes and chocolate all day. Then Tim arrived back slightly drunk with yet another benefactor who, the next day, organized a bus to take us off to see Schliersee and the mountain castle built by mad king Ludwig of Bavaria. We left Munich amazed by the generosity of the people, heading for our fast drive through Austria into communist Yugoslavia.

Tearing through Zagreb and round Belgrade fine progress was made, until, driving through the night, something caused one of the Land Rovers to leave the road and tip over. Five of us were in the vehicle and miraculously Maggie was the only one slightly injured. She had cracked a couple of ribs.

I think the driver at the time of the accident was the bombastic Rik. A big bespectacled man with strong opinions on most matters. I never got that close to Rik, and I had the feeling that he did not have much time for me either. I was in his eyes, a hindrance, a metropolitan, arty bugger who would have difficulty changing a light bulb let alone servicing a Land Rover. He was Angus's first cousin, most certainly a competent engineer although he loudly echoed most of what Gus said anyway.

Extraordinarily, thanks to Jim, we managed to rebuild the very severely damaged Land Rover in the ensuing twelve days at a campsite near Topola around fifty miles south of Belgrade. It was a long boring interlude in our trip. Jim sounded the only alarming note. One of the worst outrages of the war occurred in nearby Kragujevac when the Germans rounded up hundreds of partisans and burned them to death in a barn. Jim was terrified of anyone finding out that he was a German. Jim was a delightful man. At 39 he was a good fifteen to eighteen years older than the rest of us, with a quiet and intelligent demeanor. Quite frankly we would never have completed the journey without him, but he remained modest and self-effacing throughout.

Finally, when autumn arrived, the expedition set off south again, round Skopje and into Greece via Thessalonica, proceeding along the northern Greek coast to Turkey and Istanbul. We should have spent some time sight-seeing in one of the world's great cities but no, this culturally blinkered group only had one thing in mind, getting to Australia as quickly and cheaply as possible. So, two nights later we set out for Asia on the ferry across the Bosphorus. I don't recall that there were any bridges back then.

The Overlanders continued into Turkey through increasingly mountainous country, camping outside Ankara, and then heading for the Black Sea coast at Samson. Then we had a nice break when Tim, the ex-naval man, spotted the British Destroyer, HMS Aisne at anchor. He managed to wangle all of us on board to have showers, lunch, and beer. The ship also produced two cartons of cigarettes. I cannot begin to explain how welcome it all was. It could only have been Tim who would take that sort of initiative. The term "control freak" had not been introduced at that time but the description would have suited him. He kept a detailed record of everything, the miles we travelled, the petrol and oil we consumed, the food, the loo paper, our cigarettes. Everything. A well-made, blond-haired man with a permanently worried look as he strode around our camp sites. He was indispensable.

Camped just outside Trabzon on the black sand beach we had our first hostile encounter with a bunch of Turkish children and teenagers who tried to stop us leaving. They had come to see us the previous evening as we sat round our campfire. Larry had a guitar and knew just one song which I believe was an Appalachian dirge called 'Once I wore my apron low.' He must have played that about twenty times at the ceaseless demand of the Turkish kids now in their hundreds. I remember that, when they appeared the next morning and threatened us if Larry didn't play it 'one more time,' it was the only time we took out the 22-bore rifle that we had hidden wrapped in oil cloth and attached to the axle of one of the vehicles. Angus decreed that we should form a line and march towards the hundred or so kids. We managed to get out in one piece.

Gus was very definitely our leader. A barrel-chested, bespectacled man who brooked no opposition, he was a strong character with a good sense of humour and considerable charm. Two years of National Service in the army had given him a sense of discipline and we somehow recognized that so we tended to fall into line when he intervened in disagreements about the next course of action.

My relationship with my fellow Overlanders was comparatively unchallenging. I did feel inadequate when it came to matters mechanical, but I drove my share of the miles we covered, and I undertook my share of the meagre cooking duties. I still felt like a bit of an outsider,

probably caused by our previous occupations.

Driving through Eastern Turkey was no picnic. The passes were steep and high, with the Kopdagi Pass at eight thousand feet. There was a brief stop in the Kurdish town of Erzurum before heading for the Iranian border right by Mount Ararat, reputedly where Noah's Ark came to rest. The Iranian border proved easier than most and we drove on via Tabriz to Teheran where the tent was erected above the city in an area called Teheran Pars.

My fellow travelers continued with their lack of interest in the historic places through which we passed. Remember that, to the core of the group, this was regarded as an automotive challenge not a sightseeing trip. Accordingly, when I mentioned, near Mashhad in northeastern Iran, that we were passing one of the most important shrines in the Muslim world, visited by twenty million pilgrims a year, no one wanted to stop. When I added that the tomb of Omar Khayyam was not far away either, I was met with a chorus of "Who?" led by Rik and Tim after which I gave up.

The Afghan border proved a problem. In fact, it was a week-long problem. Alan and I managed to get dysentery. As we were incredibly careful about treating our drinking water, it was from the dust on the roads which of course had a fair content of animal droppings: camels, sheep, goats and cattle. The dysentery experience left us so weak that we could not walk for a couple of days. Camping next to the border post for a week was one of the most unpleasant experiences I have had before or since. It was cold and the wind blew dust into everything.

Alan, who was every bit as sick as I was, was a tall, good-looking fellow with an authoritatively deep voice and a serious mien. He was also a competent mechanic and pragmatic when resolving the many arguments that we all had. I certainly found him the easiest to get on with.

The challenge of the non-existent Afghan roads was formidable, first to Herat and then south to Kandahar. The problem was due to the ongoing competition between the USSR and the USA. The Americans were trying to build a highway from Herat to Kandahar and the Russians were trying to link Kandahar and Kabul. They had both only got to the initial stages, so we were forced to drive all the way on tracks alongside. We had countless punctures and broken springs. At one stage we used wooden planks to prop up one of the springless Land Rovers until we found a garage.

This then was undeniably a wild country with some resolutely hostile-looking people. Luckily by then we did not look too friendly either. Eight bearded and filthy young men mostly around six feet tall, accompanied by two Amazons of much the same height, must have given them pause for thought. We stopped off for a while in Kabul, which back then more closely resembled a medieval city.

People have asked how eight young men behaved themselves over two months in the enforced company of two nubile young women, which necessitated occupying the same tent. Everybody behaved quite well, but it was later learned that both Mags and Sam received at least two desperate marriage proposals each from one or two of the more eager, and deluded, Overlanders.

We did however collectively experience the romance of the Khyber Pass and the Lataband Pass as the tail-end of the Hindu Kush mountain range was negotiated. It was sobering to see the badges of British and Anglo-Indian Regiments displayed on the corners of hairpin bends. They were there to remind everyone who passed by that the Afghan Pathans had wiped out several British armies during the three Afghan Wars of the nineteenth century. As we have subsequently been made aware, they still have not really been beaten by anyone.

Language had not been a consideration when we planned the drive from London to Calcutta in autumn 1962. Surely everyone would speak English. We passed through the French, German, Serbo-Croat, Greek, Turkish, Kurdish, Azeri, Persian, Dari, and Pashto languages without using any of them.

We must have been about three quarters of the way through our determinedly English-speaking journey as we dropped down from the Khyber Pass to the Afghanistan-Pakistan border and the countryside became more forgiving. Greenery was evident for the first time since leaving Europe and the mood lightened considerably. We drove on, achieving one of our longest legs until, exhausted, we pulled the vehicles off the road in the middle of fields of vivid green, ten-foot-high sugarcane. Plans were made to camp where we stopped and unloading started. From nowhere a Pathan tribesman appeared on his bicycle signaling violently that our camp could not be set up there. In our exhaustion we made to ignore him, but his frantic gesticulations persuaded us to follow him.

It was a village somewhere near the town of Jalalabad, a clean, neat place in contrast to many of the villages seen earlier. A young man, who, it turned out, was the only English speaker in the Pashto-speaking village, came forward and said,

'No one must camp near our village. You will stay in our guesthouse.'

This was the most prominent building in the village, freshly white-washed with enough scrupulously clean rooms for all ten of us. For our whole stay meals were served and attempts even to smoke our own cigarettes were headed off by the gift of a carton from the village shop.

The night we arrived the whole community was gathered in front of the headman to have the English language newspaper from Lahore read to them. The English speaker was the one who had to translate the newspaper and field the questions. The village headman was one of the most impressive people you could ever meet. He was very old, with a long white beard, penetrating blue-grey eyes (a common Pathan feature, rumoured apocryphally to come from Alexander's armies over two millennia earlier) and wore a gold turban. He had a magnificently wise and compassionate look about him. He watched us intently as we were closely questioned, through the interpreter, by villager after villager about England and our views on world news. We did not come out of that particularly well as they were much better informed than we were. Then the interpreter took us aside and said that the impressive headman used to speak perfect English but that he was now very old.

We learned that he had been an officer in the First World War, fighting for England in the trenches in northern France. He had forgotten all his English in the ensuing forty-five years, but his telling presence and air of quiet authority were clear. It was certainly not the last time to be reminded that spoken language is only part of true communication.

Reluctantly we left the village and headed for Pakistan, first stop Peshawar and then Lahore where I managed to sit on Kim's Gun. I was a Kipling devotee, and it was a highlight. Sam managed to make her mark, in addition to rebutting at least two proposals from two frustrated members of the team, by befriending a wealthy Pakistani businessman who took her off to the Kingdom of Swat for twenty-four hours. She swore that nothing untoward happened and it was just that the Pakistani gentleman was completely overwhelmed by her waist length red hair and magnificent six-foot frame. Knowing Sam as I did, I am certain that she would have dictated any terms quite forcibly.

Then over the Indian border to Amritsar, the Sikh Holy City, where we enjoyed a free overnight stay in nice clean rooms, with an excellent evening meal, in the famous Golden Temple, as part of the Sikh tradition of offering all travelers unconditional hospitality.

The next memorable experience was Agra and the Taj Mahal. At that time, the number of tourists was in the hundreds rather than the thousands. Our old army tent was spread out as a ground sheet in front of the long pool facing the building itself. We lay there in the warm Indian night under the full moon, gazing at one of the most beautiful buildings in the world and woke to see it at dawn with only a few score people around us. That was a privilege that is unlikely to be repeated by anyone. For me it was one of the outstanding memories of the whole journey.

We managed to get arrested and thrown into a police cell later in India for photographing a ferry we had to take across the Ganges. Admittedly it was a tense time as the Chinese Army was massing on the Indian border to the north and it was assumed that we had to be

Chinese spies photographing the infrastructure. We were eventually released and continued on the Great North Road all the way to Calcutta.

There were two contacts in Calcutta (now called Kolkata). The first came through connections with Tim's family and was a Scot by name of Binney Smith, one of the last of his kind involved with the once thriving jute industry, from which Dundee in Scotland grew rich. A night or two spent at Titaghur Jute Mills near Dum Dum with our host proved to be too far from the centre of Calcutta where we had to be to negotiate the next part of our journey.

It was impossible to continue overland through what was then East Pakistan, later to become Bangladesh, and Burma (later to be called Myanmar). Burma was then a no-go area, and it was under a military dictatorship, as it still is. It turned out that our vehicles could not be sold in India to raise the cost of getting out of the country, due to the carnet which would have necessitated paying around three hundred percent of the value. Having reached Calcutta our game little Land Rovers had each done around nine thousand miles averaging 135 miles a day, but through large parts of Iran, Afghanistan and Pakistan were only doing 50 to 70 miles a day.

Funds were depleting rapidly and then the marvelous Marge Lever came to our rescue. She was the wife of Joe Lever, the head of the Hong Kong & Shanghai Bank in Calcutta and lived in a large and very famous house. Number One, Hastings Park Road which, we were informed, was once the residence of Clive of India. Sam managed to get funds from home to fly out to Australia from Calcutta, Maggy flew via Bangkok to meet with us in Singapore and the rest of us bedded down on the capacious verandah encircling the first floor. We certainly outstayed our welcome and poor Marge Lever was at her wits end as to what to do with us.

Rescue arrived in the form of the Indo-Chinese War. It was a dangerous time for the world and the armed forces of the west were assembled in Singapore to be ready for a possible Chinese invasion. Two Australian frigates, HMAS Queenborough and HMAS Quiberon, were sent seventy miles up the Hooghly River to Calcutta to wave the flag and show support for India.

History does not reveal the hold that Marge Lever had over Captain Murray but very grudgingly he agreed to help get us, and our vehicles, out of India. Luckily, the ships did have deck space allocated to shore vehicles and he laid down the condition that we had to organize a floating crane and load one vehicle each under the pall of night onto each ship. Then we were to come on board, change into Australian naval rating uniforms and, overnight, paint the battered and bruised Land Rovers naval grey! We managed to do all that after negotiating the hire of a floating crane for seventy pounds and the next morning we were sailing full steam down the Hooghly.

Dangling off davits in the bright, tropical sunshine whilst we painted the sides, as the ship headed across the Bay of Bengal, did not seem too bad. As was quite common in the navy, ships sometimes stop off on an empty beach to allow the sailors to drink their heads off and relax before causing too much damage in port. The Australian navy referred to it as a 'Banyan.'

The two frigates anchored off the island of Pulau Langkawi right on the Thai/Malay border. It is now a fashionable and crowded tourist destination. Back then it was beautifully deserted until two or three hundred young Australian sailors, us included, came ashore. Fires were built, a huge amount of Fosters' Lager was consumed and the 'poms' were challenged to a game of touch rugby. Having had dysentery and driven seven thousand miles in great discomfort we were no match and were nursing bruises for days afterwards.

Five of us were thrown off in Penang and one each stayed on the ships accompanying the Land Rovers to help unload them when they got to Singapore. The two-hundred-mile journey from Penang to Kuala Lumpur was achieved in the cheapest way by us all crowding into a taxi. In Kuala Lumpur we found the best value accommodation lay in renting a room in a brothel, where noises off disturbed us throughout the night. We proceeded by train to Singapore where Gus, with his army connections, had negotiated a Nissan Hut in the British Army base, and where we were re-united with our Land Rovers and our two other travelling companions. I do recall a profound sense of achievement when we finally arrived in Singapore. It was not exactly how we had planned it but on a budget of around £180 (equivalent to around £4,700 in 2023) each we had covered 9,000 miles and survived for four months.

A stall was set up in the Chinese market and we managed to sell all the supplies, given to us by our sponsors, that were still left. That made enough to get on a boat to Australia. Miraculously the two Land Rovers were to be sold for more than we had paid for them in Norfolk, but not before I had one small adventure in Bugis Street, famous for its pavement restaurants, prostitutes, and transvestites.

It started with my ardent wish to get away for just one evening from the other six left in Singapore, after over three months of intimate living. I had had enough of fitting in with everybody. I found a bar somewhere in the Tanglin area and was drinking a beer quietly on my own when I was hailed by two burly British Naval Petty Officers with strong Portsmouth accents and accompanied by two European women whom I gathered had been left behind in Singapore from a previous era. They were just being friendly, and they had assumed from my voice that I must be a very junior officer in mufti. When they learned that I was a civilian and that I had a Land Rover, they persuaded me to take them down to Bugis Street. The T shaped street, cordoned off by military police, was crammed with thousands of soldiers, sailors and airmen from the UK, USA, Australia, New Zealand, and Canada. They were all in town waiting for the Chinese to invade India. Add to that a few hundred tarts and waiters and the place was absolutely jumping. The two Petty Officers ordered "nasi goring" – the dish you always asked for in Singapore, for us all, but when the bill came, they demurred. The Chinese waiter was having none of it and the large, well-honed POs stood up with grins on their faces ready for a fight. The fourteen-year-old waiter, for that's the age he seemed to be, held a bottle threateningly over the edge of the table. That is when all hell broke loose. I think it may have gone down as the biggest bar-brawl in history. Aussies fought Poms, Canooks fought Yanks, and everybody joined in including the Chinese waiters. I got out through a back door with the aid of one of the bar girls. On reflection (but not examination), he/she could have been a transvestite. I found the Land Rover and fled home to the Nissan hut in Tanglin.

After the vehicles were sold, enough had been raised, after Mags, Patrick and Larry flew from Singapore, for six of us to book passage on an elderly Dutch Royal InterOcean Lines tramp steamer, M.S.Siaoe, which held sufficient cabins and an intoxicated Dutch Captain. We spent Christmas at sea as the old boat ploughed its way through the Indonesian archipelago. It took weeks to get to its first stop, Newcastle in New South Wales, then to Sydney.

As we entered the Sydney Harbour Heads, on January 10th, 1963, we had a stylish ceremony to enact the sharing out of the funds we had remaining, with which to start life in Australia.

It was fifteen shillings each.

# Chapter Four

## BECOMING A DINKY-DI OZ

The long walk up from the Sydney harbour docks in the hot January sun didn't bother me that much. There was only one small cardboard suitcase to carry containing a suit, a shirt and a pair of shoes. The old tramp steamer had docked at around six in the morning and I'd made the decision not to accompany the others down to Melbourne. It wasn't that they were unlikeable, it was just that after nearly four months we had all uncovered each other's faults. The two years in the States on my own had prepared me for solo travelling.

The alternative to the long, hot walk, to take a taxi, was not sensible with just fifteen shillings worth of coins jingling in my pocket. The destination, predictably for the third time in my life, was the YMCA in downtown Sydney.

'Do you have a room? I'm afraid I don't have any money...?' The look from the reception guy spoke volumes.

'What *have* yer got, mate?'

'Well...my passport ... and this suitcase?'

He snorted, 'Leave yer passport mate. You can stay three nights and owe us for the room.'

Trudging up to my very small double room, which I was to share with someone else, I could hear him muttering 'bloody pom'.

At nine in the morning, three hours after landing, I headed off to Sydney's largest department store, David Jones, and asked to see the Personnel Department. Twenty minutes later I was selling men's underwear on the ground floor at seventeen pounds a week. Around ten a.m. it was up to personnel again.

'I can't think of any other way to put this, but if you don't advance me some wages, I may not live to see the week out. I only have fifteen bob on me.'

The unspoken look again said, 'bloody pom', but the advance was ten pounds and just before noon I made for the nearest pub in the heart of Sydney. The pub was empty save for the rough-looking barman with his sleeves rolled up over his shoulders and an assortment of tattoos on his formidably muscular arms.

'Please may I have a beer,' in my most refined and polite voice.

He totally ignored me. I repeated myself. Still nothing. I rapped a coin on the counter and started to speak again. He was across the bar in a flash grabbing my shirt front and pulling me towards him.

'Go back to bloody England you f'ing pom'.

It was my first lesson in how not to talk to Australians. He thought I was patronising him by being polite. I should have said, 'G'day mate, gissabeerwillya'.

Back at the David Jones department store I sold Y-fronts diligently to the middle-aged wives who bought underwear for their husbands. In my lunch hours over several weeks I tried to get appointments with every advertising agency in Sydney to get back on track with my fledgling career. I received another vital slice of education in Australian manners at Palm Beach in North Sydney. I shared a room at the Y with an American from Kentucky who was bumming around the world. He knew a few more people in Sydney than I did, which wasn't too difficult as I knew none. He told me that he could conjure an invitation to a party up in Palm Beach, a northern suburb of Sydney.

The party was in full swing when we got there. I was not aware that human beings like this inhabited our planet. They were all coloured a deep mahogany with straw-coloured hair bleached with lemon juice and Ajax cleaner (as I understood later). The men were magnificently athletic, but it was the girls who were really spectacular. I think the word is 'built'. I had never seen women like this before, but they certainly weren't crowding round me. I sat on the floor, my back to the wall, and watched these visions as I morosely downed beer after beer. One of the surfies stared down at me.

'What are you looking at, mate?'

I mumbled something, stood up and received a push across the room. Something snapped, and I tried drunkenly to swing back. The next I knew I was semi-conscious on the floor.

'For Pete's sake give him a beer. I could be bloody wrong, but I reckon that was a Pom trying to fight back. Good on 'im'.

The moral: get your punch in first.

After a few weeks, in which time I had moved to a bedsit in Edgecliff, my perseverance paid off. It was just as well because I was leading a fairly lonely existence in Australia's largest city. At Australia's then largest ad agency, USP Benson, many years later to become Ogilvy's and part of the giant WPP group, there was the unexpected offer of a job in Melbourne. They flew me down to start as the Assistant Account Executive on the Shell Account. There was no choice but to be re-united with my Overlanders.

Gus, Rik, Alan, Jim and Pat had all ended up in a spacious bungalow in Malvern Road, Toorak, the southern and less salubrious end of the smartest suburb in Melbourne. They were still dressed ready for changing the oil in the Land Rovers and they were still arguing amongst themselves, but oh how I welcomed their company after my time in Sydney.

On reflection this might have been the worst thing that I could have done. For once I'd made an independent, and what might even be described as a courageous decision, to strike out on my own in Sydney. The job offer was indeed great, and I probably had no choice but to accept it. However it threw me back into the group and I was just a crew member again. My brief foray into developing my own independence was temporarily halted.

Social life hadn't altogether taken off, but two spots proved a good source. The Fawkner Club Hotel was a pub in South Yarra maybe ten minutes from our house. It was a functional place, fully tiled for hosing down after the six o'clock swill and with a lively beer garden. It was crammed on Fridays and Saturdays and pretty full the rest of the time. There was no food of any description. The routine was simple and, with six o'clock pub closing times back then in Victoria, had to be totally efficient. If you were drinking with five others in your 'school' the first one in would order twelve 'middies' (a bit less than a half pint), put them on the shoulder high shelf positioned on the tiled wall behind you and wait for your mates. In they would come, reach behind you, swallow the first one in a single gulp and halfway through the second glass would greet you with a 'G'day, mate'. This way you could be sure of getting in at least six to ten rounds in the hour or so reluctantly allowed by the State of Victoria. At around half-past six it was carnage, with drunken fights and the highest single-hour car-crash statistics recorded anywhere in the world. The jack-booted Victorian police, chosen largely for their size, sadistic behaviour and athletic ability saw heavy action outside most popular pubs.

The other social spot was the Treble Clef Coffee Bar in Toorak Road. It was considered quite a civilised, genteel place to meet and generally was, until the Overlanders pitched up. There was a girl in the group singing there, with whom Rik had fallen hopelessly in love. She was Judy Durham, and the group were The Seekers just starting off on their amazing career. We were amongst their most devoted early fans and got to know them really well. I somehow doubt they'd remember us now.

What really enhanced out social life was the drinking den at Malvern Road. We let it be known down at the Fawkner that if ten or twelve middies weren't enough in the hour and a half allotted, they could always get more down at the Poms' house in Malvern Road. We ran a trust bar uniquely stocked just with bottles of Fosters and our new-found best mates would come in and put an 'x' by their name and settle up every week. We were never cheated, and I think we had about thirty names on that list. The empty bottles were stacked along the forty-foot garden fence and when that was completed, we'd ring the 'bottlo', an honoured public servant in Victoria, who would come every couple of weeks to take them away. Our social life grew exponentially.

Looking back in time I realise that this combination of the pub and the drinking den was where I got into the *habit* of drinking. I'm not sure that, at this stage, it could be called alcoholism, but the habit almost certainly laid the foundations for addictive behaviour later on. If I had just been more aware and had broken the endless succession of drunken evenings by choosing not to turn up at the pub for maybe two or three nights in the week that might just have stopped me being habituated.

Eventually Alan Stewart and I decided that we had to make the break from the group, and we found a flat up in South Yarra in a modern block in Tivoli Place. Life in Melbourne got much better and as we were both keen skiers, we had to try the slopes. Unfortunately, we chose the nearest skiing place to Melbourne. It was Mount Baw Baw and had a rope-tow ski-lift and precious little else. On the way up through the Victorian gum forests in Alan's little red mini we hit a wombat. The wombat just shook itself a couple of times but the mini was nearly written off.

Then someone told us that Baw Baw was not Australia's answer to Zermatt and that we should try Mount Buller, Hotham and Falls Creek. That advice was to open up a whole new circle of friends and great weekends. It turned out that the snow-covered area of Australia between June and September was larger than the whole land area of Switzerland. As the highest point in Australia was Mount Kosciuszko, at just over seven thousand feet, and the temperatures were never really low enough, the quality of the snow was not too good. The partying however more than compensated.

At that time Mount Buller was really just a collection of privately owned chalets and a couple of modest functional restaurants. I don't remember a hotel. The chalets were usually built by consortia of generally young Melbournians through the summer months. Alan and I managed to get into one such consortium and went on a couple of working weekends to justify our participation in the winter. I do remember that you had a thirty-minute walk from the car park up to the resort in all weathers carrying your case and skis.

We were both reasonably good skiers, so we met up with other skiers who were generally much better than us, including some of the top racers and Olympic skiers. We weren't as good, but we managed to keep up and got on well with most of them. The snow was generally rather wet and sticky, the pistes weren't groomed as they are today, and the lift system was primitive with mostly T bars, but we enjoyed every minute of it. We also ended up going to Mount Hotham and Falls Creek, the other two main resorts in the Victorian Alps.

Alan met up with Sherry, a gorgeous, funny and influential girl who introduced him to the more glittering side of Melbourne society. Most of these people had houses down at Portsea, right at the end of Melbourne Bay, an idyllic spot with wide beaches. I somehow managed to get caught in his wake and spent many memorable weekends down there.

In the ground-floor of our South Yarra flat lived two other men who were to become good friends of ours, Malcolm 'Pongo' Hill and Duncan Harris, who was sometimes referred to as 'Drunken Duncan'. In point of fact he was no more drunken than I was, but it was a nickname that rolled off the tongue in your early twenties in Australia. He was another junior account executive at USP Benson and on his weekends was a semi-professional Australian Rules footballer for Bairnsdale, one of the teams in the 'Bush League'. He was a big athletic fellow and appeared to be enjoying life hugely.

Later on in the proceedings Alan got engaged to Sherry and for some reason moved out of our flat in South Yarra (maybe he went home to England for a short while, but I can't actually remember). When Duncan also moved out, 'Pongo' moved up to share with me.

By then I too had found love – with Jenny. I have nothing but great memories of Jenny and if I had been a lot more grown-up and drunk a lot less, I think we might even have remained together. She was blonde, very attractive and vivacious and I just took her for granted which was a great shame.

We used to get up parties of six to eight and go off 'into the bush' for hilarious weekends. It started up at Jenny's parents' hometown of Mount Macedon, north of Melbourne. At midnight after a roast dinner we called a 'ring-in' radio programme on the local radio station known as 'the greater 3UZ'. For some reason the disc jockey thought we'd be an attraction on his programme, and he christened us 'the Macedon Mob'. Every weekend thereafter, we would phone in from wherever we were, after a slap-up dinner, mostly drunk. We called from somewhere down on the Great Ocean Road. We called from Bairnsdale. We called from Wagga Wagga. We called from Buller.

From Ballarat. From Deniliquin. We covered the whole of Victoria and into New South Wales. The disc jockey started to build his programme round our performance at midnight.

'We should be hearing from the Macedon Mob in a minute or two. Wonder where they've got to this weekend?'

We became an institution.

One unforgettable weekend up in southern New South Wales it was decided that kangaroo shooting on horseback would be a diversion. Frankly I was uneasy round horses and wasn't really able to ride. This was to be done bareback carrying a rifle. The weary looking old horse had gone about fifty yards out of the paddock when it took off and deposited me on the ground. I'd broken my wrist. The others returned reluctantly and surveyed me from horseback.

'Geez, Fitz, can't you even stay on, you miserable bastard?'

One of them got off and saw that I was in considerable pain. He went over and got an old bit of fence post and a cleaning rag and rigged up a splint. He handed me a couple of cans of Fosters and said 'Stay in the shade mate. We'll be back in a few hours.'

He got back on his horse, and they all rode off to shoot 'roos. The drive back to Melbourne took about five hours and we stopped frequently at pubs to keep me anesthetised. Back at Melbourne General the admissions nurse told me to wait three hours to sober up before I could be treated.

There was one weekend when Duncan and I were seeing a friend off at Port Melbourne on an Italian ocean liner heading for Genoa via Adelaide. This friend had managed to print fake boarding passes. We naturally assumed that this was because he did not really want to leave his friends behind. Duncan and I reached a mutual decision to stay on till Adelaide and continue the party in the friend's cabin. We wandered around the ship's decks for a few hours and then Duncan accidentally cut himself on a broken glass and bled profusely. There was an attempt to hide but, in the end, we were hauled before the irate Italian Captain. He threatened to lock us up for the three weeks attempting to accuse us, quite wrongly, of breaking the glass on a fire alarm which he alleged had caused Duncan's bleeding. He announced that he would transport us to Genoa and then have us arrested for endangering the ship's safety. He eventually relented and threw us off at Adelaide. Our friend Maurice 'Chips' Chippendale who had the sense to leave the ship before it sailed in Melbourne had very sportingly agreed to drive the five hundred odd miles to Adelaide to pick us up.

'That's what mates are for' intoned Duncan.

As we had to be at work on Monday morning, we were badly inconvenienced by running out of petrol near Ballarat and had to push the car, for what seemed like hours, to a petrol station. How we got into our respective workplaces on Monday morning is still mystifying.

I had dived into Australia. I loved the lifestyle, the totally irreverent humour, the way Australians could insult you in two hundred different ways, the way people didn't take themselves seriously, the sport, the sun, the Olympian beer drinking. I also managed to get near my short-term career goal by becoming a copywriter at USP Benson, but the fact remains that nearly all activities ended up with a lot of drink being consumed. My social and recreational life revolved around drinking to excess.

The Prime Minister of Australia was Robert 'Bob' Menzies of the Liberal Party who was to 'reign' from 1949 to 1966. He had also been Prime Minister for two years during World War Two. 'Pig-iron Bob' could do no wrong and in a sense, he was Australia's Churchill figure. He presided over a conservative, quite narrow-minded and rather bigoted country when it came to Asians, perhaps understandably, bearing in mind their experiences with Japan in the war. Nowadays the Asian population is well over ten percent of the roughly twenty-five million inhabitants. Also, there is significant external land investment from China and Japan.

Bob Menzies was succeeded by the short-lived Harold Holt, who had an extraordinary tragic connection with my flatmate Alan Stewart in 1967. Alan had been in a car accident in which his fiancée Sherry Gillespie had died. Her parents very loyally treated Alan as part of the family thereafter and Harold Holt was a good friend of theirs. Alan was walking on the beach at Portsea on his own with Australia's Prime Minister who had told his bodyguards to take a break. Holt walked into a turbulent sea with Alan protesting nervously that perhaps he should not go in when there was nobody else around. The Prime Minister retorted that he had been swimming in these waters all his life. Alan never saw him again. He waded in but there was nothing Alan could do as Holt had disappeared completely in the rough seas. The world's press descended on Portsea and the Gillespies hid Alan away in their house for weeks. One night, Alan, desperate to escape, got in his mini and drove off at night to meet other friends. Some press reporters followed him and drove him off the road. Alan was in a coma for nearly six weeks. Nearly fifty years later he is alive and well and I was to stay with him in Australia on a visit in early 2017.

Australia in the early sixties was often regarded by the rest of the world as a conservative, cultural desert. I can't say that I did much to unearth the cultural side of Australia, but I suspect that it was an unfair judgement. It was a tremendous mix of then almost exclusively European origin, save for the half-million Aboriginal peoples who at that time led a miserable existence. Melbourne was reputed to be the largest Greek city in the world after Athens and the largest Yugoslav city after Belgrade. In fact, on one extraordinary weekend there was a pitched gun battle in Melbourne Market between Serbs and Croats, pre-dating the Balkan Wars by nearly thirty years.

At that time, unbeknownst to me, a whole lot of really good Australian writers and artists started to appear, and one great memory was of seeing Margot Fonteyn and Rudolf Nureyev and the very talented Australian Ballet company in 'Giselle'. Actually, part of that memory was watching Nureyev, who had only defected from the USSR earlier that year, do a series of leaps that were breathtakingly athletic, in that he must have been fully extended at least six feet in the air as he circled the stage. The leaps were met with wild applause from the Australian audience who, I suspected at the time, were secretly thinking how good he could have been at Australian Rules football. There was a film out at that time about Aussie Rules called *And the Big Men Fly*.

It was wildly boring being a be-suited messenger boy on the Shell account. I didn't get much joy out of delivering, or, on occasions, even selling other people's ideas. I impressed on everybody I bumped into that I could really make a great copywriter. My wish being eventually granted, I was put under the charge of one Bill Patey who announced that I was the worst writer he'd ever come across. He made me write and re-write the body copy of a sixty-four-page booklet solely devoted to barbed-wire fencing which was obviously addressed to quite a big market in a country with thousand-square-mile properties. It took about a month to get it finally accepted. Another three months passed by before any ad I wrote even saw publication. It was the best training I could ever have had. A few months after that I was headhunted by a small independent Melbourne ad agency as the copy chief, not difficult as I was the only writer.

It was in Australia that the prevalent drinking culture started to take hold of me. Your peers judged you by the amount you could drink before falling over. It was a source of endless humour, and you weren't really accepted, or so I thought, unless you could hold your drink, which had to be consumed in fierce quantities. We drank at The Fawkner, we drank at the Botanical, we drank at Jimmy Watson's Wine Bar (six pence a glass I recall), we drank on the road, and we drank at home. Then my first car crash occurred. My delightful girlfriend went by the way. I started to feel restless. Maybe Australia wasn't big enough for me.

By this time my new flatmate was Malcolm Hill, known universally as Pongo. He was an endearing fellow and a good friend but could never be described as intellectually curious. He spent much of his time reading comics and watching television. He was originally an Englishman who had lied about his age and come over to Australia as a sixteen-year-old jackaroo, but he was now undeniably an Aussie. He told chilling stories about working on a vast station (ranch) in West Australia as the only employee. Although not particularly tall, the experience had certainly made him physically tough and immensely strong. The odd time when we did manage an intelligent conversation, when I was near sober and he had dragged himself away from the Beano, we got to talking about another overland trip. That's when the idea of driving through Africa was formed.

Driving through the Americas was initially a strong contender but, in the end, it was decided that making our way overland through

Africa, from south to north, would not only be easier but cheaper. Pongo and I didn't really have much idea about Africa. I at least, knew roughly where the various countries were placed on the map, but I don't think Pongo had a clue nor cared less. I did know that the Congo in 1965 was best avoided but other than that it remained the Dark Continent.

Australian cultural requirements dictated that leaving from Australia meant that the most important decision was the location of the farewell party and the invitation list. Both these decisions were taken out of our hands by the ever resourceful Drunken' Duncan. We were booked to go from Melbourne to Durban on the *SS Southern Cross*, a Shaw Savill ocean liner that took about a thousand passengers in comparative comfort.

Three or four weeks prior to sailing, in May 1965, Duncan asked us to give up our address books. The only instruction he gave, was to ensure that our luggage got delivered onboard the *Southern Cross* the night before we were to sail, very early the following morning.

We knew nothing more until, a couple of days before sailing, we were instructed to turn up at the Savoy Hotel opposite Spencer Street Station in Melbourne, carrying nothing. We arrived to find the hotel lobby a scene out of bedlam. People were fighting to get into the two or three available lifts. We were eventually recognised as being essential guests and were escorted to the top-floor penthouse. It was packed with people and music was playing loudly from a 'trad' jazz band headed by Slugger Moore, then probably one of the best-known bands in Australia and largely composed of university professors. Only in Australia would a top jazz band be made up of senior academics.

Duncan had gone through our address books with a fine-tooth comb. Everybody we had both ever known in Australia appeared to be there. There were some dubious girlfriends met early on when I first arrived. There were people I now couldn't stand. There were a lot of good friends and many passing acquaintances. I don't know how many people were there, but it was into the hundreds.

Then Duncan stood on a chair 'Quiet, yer bastards. Be sure to get your train tickets from me and then get across to Spencer Street Station. Platform Five. There's grog on board.'

The ticket was printed *'The Fitzgerald-Hill Express to Digger's Rest'*. Digger's Rest was a village on the road to the gold-mining towns of Ballarat and Bendigo. It was about thirty miles up the track from Spencer Street and in those days, trains didn't stop often in Digger's Rest. There just weren't the gold miners anymore.

We all piled on board the train specially hired by Duncan and sure enough there was a keg of Foster's Lager on tap in all of the four carriages. We set off with Slugger Moore occasionally marching his band up and down the train to keep us in the mood. On arriving at Digger's Rest everybody got out. The sole guard told us that it was just a brief stop to allow people to stretch their legs. We didn't think so. A party was started on the platform.

The station master appeared. 'Get back on the train' he screamed. 'Yer only meant to be here for five minutes.'

Then two lanky, laconic Victorian State police were summoned. They viewed the hundreds of celebrating drunks, summed up the situation quickly, took off their tunics and gratefully accepted a beer. Eventually we got back on board and the train driver, who was by then totally sloshed as well, allowed my old girlfriend Jenny to wear his hat and drive the train back to Spencer Street. Many got off at Spencer Street, but Duncan somehow persuaded the train company to allow the train to be taken down to Port Melbourne. The track ended up opposite where the *Southern Cross* was moored. Everybody piled out next to the largely darkened ship. Pongo and I stood up on a bench surveying our friends and reeling drunkenly whilst the band played *'Waltzing Matilda'*, *'Click go the Shears'*, *'Pub with no beer'*, and an assortment of Aussie songs. The lights started to go on all over the ship as people were wakened from their dreamless sleep. We were both drunkenly blubbing.

It was the best send-off ever mounted. It even made the main newspapers the next day. Good old Duncan. Good old alcoholic habit-forming Australia.

# Chapter Five

## EXPLORING AFRICA IN A PANEL VAN

The Southern Cross ocean liner represented untold luxury to two unattached males in their early twenties. All the food you could eat, bars open all hours and even the occasional unattached girl under sixty. I think it took about two weeks to get to Durban with a stop off at Fremantle, Western Australia for a night. I managed to meet a South African girl on her way home which made the journey more fun for me but irritating for Pongo. We did however meet up with two young Americans, Jim and Bill. They were a laid-back couple of mid westerners dressed in jeans and khaki. One was bearded but not to the degree of my friend Pongo, who could barely find his mouth and nose. They had been circling the globe one step ahead of the US draft board which was trying to get them to join in the Vietnam War, as 1965 was the year that American combat troops were first landed there. They had great tales to tell and appeared to have gone to every country in Asia including North Korea whilst not setting foot in either North or South Vietnam. They were, like us, committed travellers and excited at hearing that we were planning to drive through Africa. We explored various ways that they could join us and settled on a fair way of splitting the costs.

Landing in Durban we set about finding a vehicle. We bought a Volkswagen panel van off an Indian pharmacist in Durban. It was pretty old and looked its age, but it seemed to go alright; the engine sounding like an old Singer sewing machine. A platform was built in the back and with some old mattresses it was soon capable of sleeping three on top and one underneath with the luggage. It was not the best way to spend the night. After a couple of months, it was a disgusting way to spend the night.

We decided to explore a bit of Natal, went up to Pietermaritzburg and then stayed with some sugar farmers near Mtubatuba on the way to the Hluhluwe Game Reserve, which was then famous for southern white rhinos, the largest of the world's five different species of rhino.

In 1965 the country we landed in was firmly under the control of the Nationalist and predominantly Afrikaans government headed by Hendrik Verwoerd. The hated apartheid system was in full swing. It was just a few months after Nelson Mandela, Thabo Mbeki, Walter Sisulu and others had been jailed for life at the Rivonia Trial. The homelands policy was in force allowing for Africans in their millions to be forcibly returned to their 'homelands'. The rest of the world condemned it but ironically it provided a safe environment for us to drive through South Africa. We were not even aware of the current political quagmire.

We headed southwest for Cape Town and found accommodation with a friend of Pongo's father who had been a senior naval officer and ended up staying at Simonstown which was then the British naval base shared with the South African navy on the Cape Peninsula. Our host in his capacity as an ex-matelot endeared himself to us by taking us to a raucous seaman's club called the Navigator's Den. It, in common with the Smuggler's Cove in Durban, (which we also visited), was famous as a place that chose not to obey the oppressive apartheid laws. Back then, ladies of the night of all colours and sailors from all over the world intermingled. We were impressed by the choice of our middle-aged host.

It was hard leaving Cape Town, knowing that our comfortable beds would be exchanged for the smelly old van, but we had places to see and people to sponge off. We made our way through the Karoo and via Bloemfontein to Johannesburg. In those days the Nationalist government kept firm law and order and the hated apartheid system kept Africans under strict control. The risk of severe punishment kept any assaults on, or thefts from, whites to a minimum. We were safe sleeping in our van.

On the way up to Johannesburg we headed for Maseru the capital of Basutoland, a tiny land-locked British colony which got its independence and became Lesotho in 1966. The King of Basutoland was Bereng Seeiso, titled Moshoeshoe II. I had been at school at Ampleforth with this King, where he had been given the politically incorrect nickname of Bongo, which didn't seem to bother him at the time. At that stage in our lives in North Yorkshire he was probably the only African any of us had ever seen. I thought it best not to use the nickname when I visited him in his corrugated iron roofed 'palace' which was quite substantial and well-furnished, but there can't have been too many kings with tin-roofed palaces. He was as charming and as self-effacing as he had been at school where he was well liked. He'd been a good tennis player and had been made a school monitor which I suppose was the least that the Benedictine monks could have done to prepare him for ruling his own country.

In Johannesburg a friend in Australia had given me the name of an up-and-coming executive in Anglo American as a contact. It just so happened that the girl I had got to know on the Southern Cross ship also worked at Anglo American. Anglo American at that time was the most important and most prestigious company in Africa. I arranged to meet Jill outside Number One, Main Street, at the offices which had wide steps leading up to the imposing, columned entrance. We parked our van right in front and the four of us got out. We weren't a very pretty sight living as we did and sleeping largely in the clothes we walked about in. Jill came prettily down the steps to greet us and at that time pointed out my 'rising young executive' contact, Drummond Campbell who was walking up the steps with a couple of senior looking and exquisitely smart executives. I approached him.

'Morning. I'm Anthony Fitzgerald. Sally Paterson in Melbourne said I should look you up'.

They all stopped and looked at the unshaven, jean clad figure in front of them. The senior men hurried on and poor, pin-striped Drummond stammered.

'Would you mind calling me later? I'm rushing to a meeting.'

You could see that any admission of familiarity with people like us might damage his career irreparably. He ran away up the steps. Whilst in Johannesburg I was never able to get through to Drummond, but I was to meet him again in different circumstances.

The next country on the route was Rhodesia, shortly to make a unilateral declaration of independence in November 1965 under Prime Minister Ian Smith. It was of course previously Southern Rhodesia, but they dropped the 'Southern' just before we arrived. Luckily, we entered and left just a few months before UDI. Rhodesia then had around half a million Europeans, and it was a prosperous, flourishing country, for the whites anyway. There was no apartheid regime as in South Africa and race relations in general were good although the whites controlled around eighty percent of the good farming land. In 1980 it completely overthrew the colonial ties and became Zimbabwe. Something had to give and as we now know it certainly reversed itself under Mugabe. In 2012 there were about thirty thousand whites remaining, just five percent of the 1965 figure.

Our first stop was the seventeen-hundred-acre site of the Great Zimbabwe ruins in the south of the country. Nobody really knows definitively when these were built or indeed exactly why, but they are evidence of a sophisticated society and are thought to have been built between the eleventh and fifteenth centuries. We travelled on to the town of Umtali (now Mtwara) set in rolling, forested hills on the Mozambique border and then to Salisbury (now Harare). In Salisbury we stayed with a tobacco farmer and were taken to the world-famous tobacco auctions which were conducted at breakneck speed with the buyers accompanying the auctioneer in amongst the bales at fast walking pace.

After Salisbury we turned south to Bulawayo and visited Rhodes tomb which was just a stone slab with an inscription set on a hilltop some forty kilometres south of the city. The next stop, driving through the Wankie Game Reserve, then alive with big herds of elephants, was Victoria Falls and the Zambian border. It's hard to say much more about the Victoria Falls other than that they are one of the world's most dramatic sights. You can only stand and stare in awe, and in silence, mainly because you can't hear yourself speak for the roar of the falling water.

On to Lusaka in Zambia and then northeast to the Tanzanian border in the direction of Dar-es-Salaam, a drive of some fourteen hundred miles of 'MMBA', 'Miles and Miles of Bloody Africa' as the local whites used to say. Zambia, previously Northern Rhodesia was declared independent in October 1964 under Kenneth Kaunda. It was always a much richer country than Southern Rhodesia because of the huge copper mines on the Congolese border. You will notice that we were travelling through southern Africa at a pretty momentous time but, I would have to confess that our north bound panel van remained largely oblivious as it rattled on through the continent.

The need for a drink had not really surfaced, even after the habits picked up in Australia. I was busy trying to achieve something and we didn't have any spare money. But I have to reflect that it was only a pause. There was nobody to challenge me and make me feel on the periphery so no need to hide from anything.

The four occupants of the panel van got on pretty well and fortunately it gave us no mechanical trouble whatsoever despite hundreds of miles of rough, corrugated 'murram' (red dirt) road. We slept in the back without trouble although I have to say that it was probably because we'd got used to the squalor. A casual visitor to the van might have viewed it, and smelled it, differently.

The only trouble we ever had at a border was crossing from Zambia to Tanzania where all sorts of objections were raised. An extra entry fee was negotiated, and we were allowed to carry on. 'Carrying on' was certainly the right description for the thousand miles of featureless bush and rough, untreated and heavily corrugated road to Dar es Salaam via Dodoma. It was an incredible relief to arrive at the Indian Ocean and swim in the sea, if only to get clean. The next leg via Arusha to Nairobi in Kenya was at least scenic and offered some variety.

Tanzania was under the presidency of Julius Nyerere and consisted of the old German colony of Tanganyika and the island of Zanzibar which came under British colonial rule after World War One and got its independence in 1962. When I later returned to live in Africa in 1968, I came to know Father John, an American priest who had been confessor to Nyerere who was a devout Catholic. I think Nyerere probably remains as the only African leader ever to retire of his own volition. He had some bizarre socialist ideas about persuading African farmers to unite in huge villages and have collective farms, Russian style. It was known as Ujamaa, did not suit the personality of the African farmer, and failed miserably. He did however do the country a great service by making them all speak one language well; the lingua franca of East Africa is Swahili and only in Tanzania is it spoken uniformly.

Pongo and I decided that we'd climb Kilimanjaro on the Kenya-Tanzania border in a day, and we made our way up to the hotel situated within the Mount Kilimanjaro National Park. There was an appealing bar and as we hadn't had a cold beer for a while we stopped there. We had several more beers and, in our shorts, and a mood of optimism, we set off for the heavily forested bottom slopes on our own, both rather too well fortified by cold Tuskers. Around three hours later exhausted and sober we had climbed maybe fifteen hundred feet and come through the dense forest. We reached the next plateau which consisted of typical mountain scrub. The clouds then parted, and we had a good view of the mountain peak in all its glory and realised to our shock that it was still at least ten miles away and a lot higher, with probably over ten thousand feet to climb. It was also a lot colder and suddenly it didn't seem such a good idea to continue. We learned later that it took a reasonably well-equipped and suitably clothed group around five days to get to the summit. Not for the first time did we feel ill-informed and suitably stupid. After all we only had to ask.

I remember staying with a Tanganyikan settler white family near Mount Meru on the way to Arusha and before heading north into Kenya. Apparently the last of the von Trapp family, of 'Sound of Music' fame still had a farm nearby. In Nairobi our contacts were surprisingly limited and thus, for the fourth time in my life I ended up staying at the YMCA. I have seriously considered calling this book 'Ys I have known around the world'.

Kenya, under Kenyatta, had been independent since 1963 and the Mau Mau uprising, which took place between 1952 and 1960, was long over. Independent Kenya may have become but there was still a large tranche of white European 'settlers' who behaved as though independence had never happened.

We met up with a fellow called Terry Tory, which sounds more like a cartoon character, who was extremely kind to us and as one of the leading Kenyan Rugby players introduced us to the Nondescripts Rugby Club where we repeatedly drank too much. We were in the company of fellow British in large and rowdy numbers. No way was I going to stay sober in that company. They might think I was boring.

It now makes sense that my habitual need for another drink was forcibly subdued by the need to drive through Africa, reaching our destination and having absolutely no spare cash. On the two occasions when we did stop to drink, I certainly didn't hold back.

We said goodbye to Jim and Bill, our American travelling companions and set about planning the next stage of our trip.

Pongo was adamant that we would drive on through Uganda and Sudan into Egypt and make our way overland all the way to Cairo. One particularly drunken evening I was forced to point out to him that, if he'd ever read a newspaper or listened to the news, he would realise that the civil war in southern Sudan was rampant and that five journalists had been killed in the past couple of months. The Shifta wars against ethnic Somalis in Kenya's NFD (Northern Frontier District) further prevented us going via Ethiopia and the Congo was completely out of the question. Over our supper in the 'Y', still feeling the effects of a convivial evening at the rugby club, I poured on the sarcasm. The next thing I knew was that Pongo, in his frustrated fury, had laid me out cold with one punch. Unfortunately, he did it across the table and the whole table, the food on it and Pongo, tipped over on top of me. We were the only 'mzungus' (Europeans) staying at the 'Y', and it was full of earnest university educated Africans in ties and collars and smart suits. They rose as one, clutching their plates and backed against the wall all round the dining room. Pongo and I had most definitely disgraced the place but as we lay on the floor, covered in ham and eggs, we both laughed at the scene around us. Peace was restored.

The only thing left to us was to drive to Kampala in Uganda stopping to view the Murchison Falls where the White Nile starts on its way out of Lake Victoria. Kampala was an attractive little city, not so little now, built on seven hills like Rome. The country, independent since 1962, was run by Milton Obote who of course was much later, in 1971, overthrown by Idi Amin.

In Kampala by extraordinary coincidence we managed to sell the trusty panel van to another pharmacist, and an Indian one at that. Unbelievably it still had its South African number plates which I would imagine the chemist arranged to change very quickly indeed. Running short of funds as usual we just about raised enough from the vehicle sale to buy an air ticket from Kampala to Khartoum.

Sudan, independent since 1952 and previously Anglo-Egyptian Sudan, was, when we visited it, in the throes of an endless civil war mainly in the south which was one good reason for overflying it. There was no visible sign of the civil war in Khartoum and absolutely no sign of any change, possibly since the Battle of Omdurman in 1898, in the hallowed halls of the Sudan Club. Against all odds they allowed Pongo and I to stay at this exclusive club before catching the train to Wadi Halfa which we had thought was leaving the next day. Catching is probably too strong a word because it turned out that a backward tortoise could have caught it. The trains ran weekly, and one had just left the day we arrived. We had a whole week in the Sudan Club, and we appeared to be the only people staying in this last bastion of British colonialism. The food was standard British prep school but perfectly passable. The trouble was that there was absolutely nothing to do, and the temperature hovered in the low hundreds. The inactivity was really getting to us, so we asked the Club Secretary if we could play on one of the totally empty and perfectly groomed clay tennis courts.

'I'm not sure about that' he harrumphed 'Do you have tennis whites?'

'We've been driving through Africa' I replied, 'Unaccountably they are not the first things we thought of packing.'

'Well, maybe I can find you some, together with rackets' he said rather grudgingly.

We sauntered out to the courts in the cool of the late afternoon with the temperature dropping to the high nineties to find two huge, coal-black Nubians in long, brilliant white djellabas and fezzes. They were situated each side of the net, next to tables on which sat large pitchers of freshly made lemonade. Their sole function was apparently to supervise and keep us watered. It was one of the strangest games of tennis I have ever experienced. Other than that, we wandered around Khartoum and Omdurman, but the heat discouraged us considerably. After six days we boarded the train, certainly well rested but stultifyingly bored.

The train had four separate classes and we plumped for fourth class which consisted largely of standing in, and occasionally lying down in the corridor. The journey to Wadi Halfa, at the north end of Lake Nasser, was the best part of twenty-four hours across the Nubian Desert. It was hellishly uncomfortable but preferable to the boredom of the Sudan Club.

It was thus more than cheering when we discovered two French girls on the train. They had been teachers in Madagascar and had got on in Khartoum. Amazingly they spoke worse English than my French, which was a lot stronger than it is now, and I undertook to translate for them on the journey to Cairo and beyond.

In Wadi Halfa at the northern end of the three-hundred-and-forty-mile Lake Nasser we boarded a boat which terminated at the Aswan Dam. This was not a luxury cruise. It was a functional ferry, and it took from memory around thirty-six hours. We were advised, that if we wanted to live, we should buy our own food and water before boarding. We slept in the open on the deck. I talked a lot of French to the two girls. It wasn't too arduous an undertaking.

Our destination was Luxor and we stayed in a run-down hotel there but managed to see almost all the sites including the Valley of the Kings, the Valley of the Queens and Karnak. In those days the number of tourists was very limited, and we were lucky enough never to be in the company of more than ten to twenty other people. I understand that nowadays it can be many hundreds. We were so lucky to be travelling the world at this time.

On to Cairo, a mad and magical city. I loved its chaos and cheerfulness. Under President Nasser Egypt was between wars and was generally welcoming to foreigners. We stayed in yet another run-down hotel, visited the huge Cairo markets, the Cairo Museum and of course the Pyramids and the Sphinx where inevitably we rode camels in the desert. By this time Pongo and I were almost always disagreeing although he never resorted to knocking me out again. When he announced that he was going to get to Europe by picking up a boat in Alexandria and go via Greece, I elected to go with the French girls to Port Said on the boat they were planning to catch. Pongo and I said goodbye and agreed to meet at my parents' house in Seillans in the Var, in the south of France, at some indeterminate time.

The girls were booked with first class tickets on a Messageries Maritimes ship bound for Marseilles. It had started in Madagascar and then the island of Reunion and doubled as a troop ship for Malagasy and Reunion conscripts for the French army. The ship was basically a ship of two halves: a luxury liner and a troop ship. I managed to get a berth in the troop ship part at a total cost of ten pounds to get from Suez to Marseilles. Sleeping in a three-tiered bunk in a large area containing many hundreds of young conscripts from Malagasy and Reunion, it had the benefit of just a handful of loos, and we ate communally below decks. However, all was not lost, and I still had my smart suit, shirt and tie in a little suitcase and, every evening, I would change in one of the revolting loos and make my way stealthily up to the first-class area where my French girls would make sure that I dined well at their table. It was a great arrangement for ten pounds and was hilariously capped when, just out of Marseilles, I was invited to dine, as the only Englishman on board, at the Captain's Table.

In Marseilles I set off for my parents' house in Seillans which was about one hundred miles to the east just above Draguignan in the Var. I had just enough money to take a series of buses and then hitchhiked from Draguignan. I was driven down to La Rouviere by Mme Magail, with her husband, the owners of the garage my parents used. My mother came out of the house and ran towards me, arms outstretched to greet once again, her returning prodigal.

*Marjorie Fitzgerald, Anthony's mother (sometime in the 1940's.)*

*Anthony Fitzgerald at 21.*

*Gus, Sam and Anthony on Afghan 'road'.*

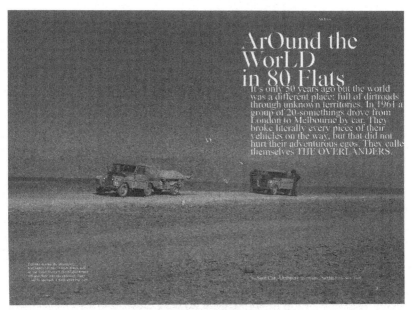

*Overlanders US Magazine article.*

*Maggie, Larry, Sam & Gus – Pakistan 1962.*

*Anthony in Sydney 1962.*

*Party time in Melbourne 1964.*

*Anthony's business partner in Kenya,
Guy Elkins 1968.*

*Anthony collecting firewood on honeymoon,
Mt. Marsabit 1969.*

*Anthony with rhinos 1972.*

*Roseanne featured in 'Hola', Buenos Aires 1971.*

*Roseanne around 1973.*

*MaryAnne, Petra & Tara.*

*Tara, Pia, Petra, Sophie, Nicky, Roseanne, Marjorie 1995.*

*Time Magazine colleagues 1992.*

*Leaving card from Time Magazine 1994.*

*Anthony with granddaughter Mia 2014*

*Philippe Marquézy, our French business partner 2000-2020.*

*Anthony with grandson Felix 2022.*

# Chapter Six

## EMBRACING SIXTIES LONDON LIFE

After a month of being spoiled in the south of France I made my way back to London to look for a job and for somewhere to stay. Confident enough to market myself as a copywriter in London, I got a job at Everett's in Victoria quite quickly. Everett's was a medium sized agency whose copywriting department had the reputation of being a 'poet's corner'. There were agencies like that still left in London and, in hindsight, it probably wasn't terribly flattering, although at the time we thought it was. The implication being that the writers were more interested in creating literary prose rather than actually selling anything, as they were paid to do. After all F. Scott Fitzgerald, Salman Rushdie, Dorothy L Sayers, William S.Burroughs, Alec Guinness, Bob Newhart, Joseph Heller and Ogden Nash had all been advertising copywriters. The London ad agency scene was really quite civilised in those days. Certainly the arrogant perception of those in the industry was that it was a gentlemanly and civilised way to earn a living. I'm not sure that the rest of society shared that opinion, unless you measure civilisation by length of lunch and conversations about anything but advertising. I was to work for a number of these sorts of agencies.

One campaign that we worked on at Everett's was for British Rail Ferries. The account director was an expatriate American who obviously felt that he had not explored the finer restaurants of the Pas de Calais and Normandy in sufficient quantity. He, the art director, his junior account executive and I as the writer, duly crossed the English Channel four times in a week ending up in places such as Lille, Amiens, Le Touquet and Deauville. We were thus equipped to write and design some really heartfelt advertising about the benefits of crossing the Channel by British Rail. Thus was advertising conceived in the creative sixties.

By now the country was under the premiership of Harold Wilson and was not quite so welcoming of the middle-class values that had held us together or even the upper-class values we aspired to. It saw the devaluation of sterling, the de-criminalization of homosexuality, UDI for Rhodesia and the escalation of the troubles in Northern Ireland.

On the creative side of the advertising industry as a writer or art director, the trick was to build up a portfolio and when you had been at an agency about nine months to a year you hawked the portfolio round to the firms which might be persuaded to pay you fifty percent more than you were currently getting.

My next agency was in Knightsbridge and went by the truly splendid name of Horniblow, Cox Freeman. The office was on the sixth floor of Bowater House which has since been replaced by the luxury residential building Number One Hyde Park which has some of the world's most expensive apartments. We looked out over Hyde Park, and I watched the uniformed Horse Guards passing by on the road below. On foggy mornings they would loom out of the mist in the scarlet uniforms and gleaming helmets.

The agency was considerably larger, it was later to become BBDO, and had some big-name clients. I worked in a small creative pod under an easy-going copy chief called Peter Kiernan and was assigned to partner with a feisty art director called Marty Stein who hailed from the Bronx in New York and sounded like a gangster. He was in his early forties, married to an Israeli 'sabra' and was, to my still juvenile mind, really old. He insisted on calling me 'kid'. His quick creative mind was a dream to work with though and we produced some good stuff together. His technique was to draw quick crayon sketches on the largest pads you could get and then bark out,

'Gimme some words, kid.'

He had a huge wastepaper basket, and I mean huge; it was three feet square by at least four feet deep and at the end of the day it would be filled to overflowing with our balled-up discarded ideas. It was fast and furious and fun.

At that stage we had the BP account and they had just contracted Spike Milligan to be the face of the brand, dressed in a Superman suit in BP colours of green and yellow. It sounds ridiculous now and must have cost them a fortune. I was asked to write copy for this campaign, and it had to be passed by the actor before submission. On one particular day the account executive was away, and I was asked to go round to Spike's place with the copy. I waited, for what seemed hours, ringing the bell and was told eventually to go away as he didn't want to see anybody. Apparently the mentally fragile Milligan did that a lot.

I was enjoying my life within and outside work and for some reason, I was on the 'eligible young bachelors' list which got me invitations to 'deb' dances and cocktail parties. These were in the top London hotels or in magnificent country homes and were a welcome relief from the pie and pint down at the pub. The ones I wasn't invited to in London I would contrive to crash. I imagine it was my watchful mother working her network that got me on to this list. Paradoxically, at that stage of my life, aged 24, I was very far from being eligible as a prospective husband. However, it necessitated me having to turn up to the office in a smart suit on most weekdays when my colleagues were dressed like normal copywriters and art directors. That is in jeans, shorts, African wrap-around kikois or Afghan sheepskin coats and equipped with guitars, pet poodles and other signs indicating that they were emphatically not to be confused with the despised upper-class account executives. They questioned me scornfully.

'Why are you dressed like a tailor's dummy again Fitz?'

'Because I have a social life outside this office, you boring tossers,' would be my reply.

It didn't win their approval. In any event I was off the 'deb's delight' list after just one year.

Ironically, we 'creative' people had nothing but contempt for the 'suits' as we termed the account executives. As far as we were concerned, they didn't have a brain in their heads and seemed incapable of selling our work to the clients. One day we rebelled and took all of Marty's 'scamps', the term he used for his sketches, and glued them over the entire parquet floor of the Bowater House office right up to the elevator doors. We then summoned the top management to come down and see something brilliant. They walked out and over all the 'scamps' on the way to our open-plan office, where we sat in silence. Marty said, "Now you see what it's like to walk all over our ideas". I think we all moved agencies shortly after that episode.

This led me to another agency just across the road in Knightsbridge called misleadingly LPA. I think the name was deliberately chosen to be confused with LPE (the London Press Exchange), one of the largest agencies in the UK. London Progressive Advertising, which is what it was, was chaired by the personable Mike Robinson. His philosophy was usually only to pitch for clients that reflected his enviable lifestyle exemplified by one of our clients being Krug Champagne. It was hugely amusing and was conveniently sited almost next door to a delightful wine bar in Pavilion Road which is where most of the serious work was done. I was now around 26 years old and probably should have been aspiring to more serious managerial roles in advertising, but I was in a nice comfortable, well-paid space where hedonism had overtaken ambition.

Our routine was to receive the brief from a despised account executive, acknowledge it with a sage and impassive nod and retire to the wine bar to think things over. After several days of vinous reflection the desperate account executive would be imploring us to meet his deadline and our ideas. A couple of hours before he was due to meet the client we would condescend to hand over the layout and copy, and he would depart elated and indebted. It was a deeply unfair but somehow satisfying technique to imply that we had been slavishly toiling under the midnight oil for weeks on end, and it certainly raised our worth, unless we were found out. We created a lot of mediocre advertising and one or two good campaigns but the one we were proudest of was for Save the Children. Our tiny agency had to pitch against three of the largest agencies in London, including J. Walter Thompson, and we won. The Marketing Director of Save the Children came in to award us the account and the management all lined up in suitably oily fashion. The art director and I were included in the welcome party, rather grudgingly, I thought.

A smallish, smartly dressed woman strode in, flanked by two obviously Etonian Guards Officer types who towered over her, but looked nothing but deferential whenever she spoke.

'Before we get down to work,'
she intoned in a sort of mid-Atlantic accent,
'You need to know that I earn more than anyone in this room.'
'The reason is that I am worth it.'
she added.
'I am not a soft touch.'

This pre-feminist message came across very clearly and it was a highly effective way of getting us to abandon our rather cavalier method of creativity...at least on that account.

By now I was earning good money and had moved into a house with some Australians in Godfrey Street, off the King's Road in Chelsea. It was a workable mix and as I'd known some of them from my time in Melbourne, we all got on together. However, I spent most of my evenings in a pub in Milner Street called, coincidentally, The Australian. Having been dropped without ceremony from the eligible bachelors' list after only one year it became central to my social life. It provided company, approbation, girlfriends, laughs, appalling food, deep and meaningless conversations, untold quantities of warm, English beer, an oasis that even offered banking services.

My habitual drinking was now permanently ingrained. It didn't stop me working or socialising, but it did punctuate everything. Down time was drink time and it often led to expensive mistakes like the time that I was going skiing on my own and managed to oversleep and miss the charter flight to Switzerland. I was drowning my sorrows when Ted the owner asked me why I was still in London. When I told him he asked,

'Why don't you catch the boat train from Victoria?'
'But I don't have enough money to do that.'
'How much do you need?'
'About a hundred quid" I suggested.'
He opened the till and counted it out.

'Pay me back over the next couple of months' he said.

Now that's what I call a good pub.

I have great memories of skiing holidays in Verbier with the Aussies, some of whom were Olympic standard skiers. The après ski stories from those holidays were legendary. One year we came across two Aussie dentists who were wild enough to be admitted to the group. They were called Bill and Ben and didn't ski as well as us but did ski just as fast. They were uncertified lunatics and would attempt to keep up without any skill whatsoever. One of them ended up semi-conscious in the top of a pine tree after missing a long, racing turn. We had to climb up and pull him down.

Another evening on our way out of a club we noticed that Ben had fallen, backside first, into a large, square-shaped wooden wastepaper or log basket positioned near the door. He had got wedged in a sort of 'v' shape and was blissfully asleep. We all filed past him and left him there for the night.

On another wonderful skiing day five of us, including two of the Australian ski racing team, drove at dawn from Verbier to Argentiere over the border in France. Although near Chamonix it was a little-known resort and had one long cable car up the 13,500-foot Aiguille Verte mountain, part of the Mont Blanc massif and connecting with the Chamonix lift system. That day, at the end of April, the whole mountain was covered in spring snow, a condition that allowed you to ski everywhere with ease. We didn't even take off our skis to eat lunch and came down at around six o'clock in pitch dark. We must have done well over thirty thousand feet downhill and flat out in one day. It was one of the most remarkable days of my skiing life etched into my memory.

Back in London, life was more than satisfactory. I had one very loyal girlfriend, but I can't say that I was quite as loyal. I am ashamed of that. The pattern of life didn't vary too much. A day's work creating what we regarded as masterpieces of copy to sell baked beans, cars, office equipment, railway ferries, airlines, motor tyres, tourist boards and banks. Lunch in a wine bar; down to the pub at six o'clock; occasional visits to a bistro for a seven and six penny steak if a girl had to be entertained; back for last orders; then a smidge of gambling down at the Apron Strings in Fulham Road; rounding off the evening with a nightcap or two at Da Angela's in Sydney Street; and so to bed at any time in the early morning hours.

I had a friend who was a Captain in the Irish Guards. Although later to be a Major General, he didn't demonstrate any unusual intellectual prowess, except for his ability to win at backgammon. He had contrived to learn by heart the whole of a little book of tables showing doubling dice odds at various stages of the game. He and I would play at the Apron Strings, which was mafia-owned and managed by a terrifying woman called Paula. I believe she was a White Russian. We would be playing backgammon quietly in a corner and I would receive a sharp kick under the table. That meant that an Iranian, Turk or Greek was watching us. Suddenly I would be allowed to start winning and inevitably the swarthy gentleman would grunt.

'I weell play the weener'.

My friend would nod politely and then win the game. By my calculation he would pick up another hundred or two each month to top up his meagre army pay. It was all done by the book.

Da Angela's was owned by an extremely kind, elegant and well-born Italian lady who remained blissfully ignorant of English licensing laws. It was a nice enough restaurant upstairs and a bar with a juke box in the basement. Nothing remarkable about any of that, but it was after eleven pm that it came into its own. The denizens of Chelsea discovered that Angela never closed the bar and enjoyed their company so much that, if necessary, you could have 'just one more' till four in the morning. I considered it quite normal to expect to be drinking at 2 or 3 in the morning and be effective at work the next day. It was there that, having a night cap with one of my housemates, we saw one of our skiing companions coming in with Christine Keeler, famous for bringing down the Tory government in 1963. We made to leave but she blocked our way, addressing my good-looking housemate.

'You can't leave until you give me your phone number' she purred and added

'I hear you're a doctor. I'm thinking of changing my doctor.'

Slightly sick that, as Doctor Ward, who had introduced her to Profumo in '63, had committed suicide subsequently.

My friend was in his last year at the Royal College of Surgeons and terrified of any scandal that might affect his position there on the eve of what was to become a very profitable career in later life.

'Let's get out of here, Fitz.'

he whispered hoarsely.

'First the number'

she said, positioning herself coquettishly in front of him.

'Flaxman 5364'

I volunteered on his behalf.

Sure enough she contacted my friend, and they had a brief three-week fling and we saw a bit of her at that time. Actually, she was a rather sweet person and certainly looked gorgeous.

Another casino that I used to frequent was the Casanova in Lower Park Lane. It served a particularly good breakfast and free drinks to its wealthy patrons. I used to turn up with a fiver after the pubs closed and try and spin it out until I had finished my free food and drink. I was at the roulette table and spied a greyhound which had been given the freedom of the club and was wandering around sniffing the patrons inquisitively. I leant back to pat it and the dog bit me hard on the hand. I overreacted,

'My god, can't a fellow have a drink at his club without being savaged by a dog?'

Paula who was now promoted to the rather grander Casanova and who knew me well from the Apron Strings appeared in front of me flanked by two seriously menacing bouncers.

'Leave now' she snarled 'That dog is worth more than you'll ever be.'

That dog had been the winner of the Greyhound Derby the year before. He actually stopped me gambling for the rest of my life. I never placed a serious bet in a casino again.

I was to develop a great friendship with Ian, another army officer. He liked his drink but certainly not as much as I did. He also liked girls and from his base in Aldershot would appear hopefully at The Australian. He was convinced that he was at least fifty percent Irish, and I knew I was even more. We spent many great evenings in various bistros in Chelsea and South Kensington singing Irish Rebel songs until he later discovered he was actually Welsh.

Actually in 1968 I was partly responsible for him having to leave the army. We were at a regimental ball in Colchester, and he had fixed up a cottage nearby for me and a girlfriend to stay in afterwards. Unfortunately, we managed to get so drunk, in full white tie and tails that we had to stay in his room in the single officers' quarters, as I couldn't even get the keys into the door of the little red mini that I now owned. In the morning the orderly came in, saw a completely strange couple in his Captain's bed and fled downstairs to inform the major in charge. Our sleep was interrupted again by a red-faced man bearing a notebook shouting.

'I want your name, rank and number.'

I replied weakly 'I'm not in the army. I don't have a number. Please could you leave us alone? We don't feel terribly well and there is a lady here.'

At this stage my girlfriend sat up, stark naked and saluted him.

He fled.

Unfortunately, when they finally caught up with Ian and his girlfriend in the orderly officer's room, this incident precipitated his exit from the army. I approached him later and offered to pay half the gratuity which he'd had to forfeit for 11 ½ years of service.

'Fitz, not only will I not accept but I'll be taking you out to dinner to celebrate. I should have left years ago.'

It turned out to be true, as he rose to be chairman of a major estate agency. The fact remains that my drinking spree completely changed the life of one of my greatest friends.

In the summer I would take a week or two down at my parents' lavender farm in Seillans, in the Var. It was always a great break, but the wine consumption didn't slacken. My mother was a very talented cook and hostess and she had been responsible for turning what had been a totally run-down peasant farmhouse into a wonderfully stylish yet simple haven. My half-sister Nicky was much in evidence on school holidays from St Mary's Ascot at that time. She was to be a great friend and purveyor of humour and common sense right up to the present day.

I suppose I could have gone on like this for years more but after three years my travel bug was surfacing again, and I was getting restless. Years later I was told of the term that alcoholics in AA meetings use. It's called doing a 'geographical'. No place is big enough for your restless soul. An alcoholic tells himself that he can escape his troubles by moving on. I didn't know it then but my exit from Australia was just the first of my 'alcoholic geographicals'.

Then something serious happened. I had a girlfriend through the summer of 1977. She too was a regular at The Australian, very pretty and we enjoyed each other's company. One day she informed me that she was pregnant, having assured me that she was on the pill. It also turned out that she was one of those girls who didn't show until late in the proceedings. This baby was going to be born no matter what. She was admitted to St George's Hospital, now the Lanesborough Hotel at Hyde Park Corner, and she gave birth on March 1st, 1978, to a healthy boy whom we called Simon.

She was only twenty and neither of us were considering marrying each other, or anyone else for that matter. The decision was made to have him adopted within five days after the birth. We were asked if we had any preferences about potential adopters. We both said Catholic having not behaved remotely like good Catholics. They added that they would find what was termed a *'professional class'* Catholic family in the south of England somewhere. It was a sobering time and a sad one. We both felt guilty, and I know that the girl, whom I never saw again after she fled back to Norfolk, was obviously distressed by it. That may have been the time that I started my overdue growing up process.

It would take another forty years before Simon introduced himself to me again.

It was thus a good time to be contacted by another copywriter friend, with whom I had worked in one of the agencies and was now rather successful as a creative group head at Bensons.

'You're always banging on about Africa, aren't you? And about what a whale of a time you had in Kenya, right?'

'Yeah, so what?'

'A job's come up and no one seems to want it. It's creative director in Bensons' Nairobi office'.

I was round there like a shot. I was required to work for three months as a copywriter at Bensons in London first and rather reluctantly left the forgiving fleshpots of LPA. At Bensons, I reported indirectly to the renowned creative director Francis Harmer-Brown and there too that I had to make my first commercial for the African market with Paddy Nolan. It was for White Cap Beer I seem to recall. The commercial, made in London with expatriate Africans pretending to be in a Kenyan bar, was really not very good but it was my first and, mercifully, it worked. I was to leave for Nairobi in August 1968 and of course, as in Australia, the farewell party was of great importance. The former workman's cottage in Godfrey Street, now probably worth a couple of million, just accommodated three people with a tiny living room and three bedrooms. I think something like ninety people were invited. It was a balmy evening and inevitably the party ended up in tiny Godfrey Street. The helpless neighbours mostly joined in but one of them must have called the police but, just like the cops who turned up for the party at Digger's Rest in Australia, these two knew they'd lost this one. Off came the helmets and they obligingly joined in.

Another eventful farewell, another 'geographical' exit was beginning as I boarded the day flight to Nairobi.

# Chapter Seven

## RETURNING TO AFRICA

It was so thrilling to be on a plane back to Africa, and even more exciting was the fact that someone else had requested my presence there and, furthermore, was actually paying for the flight. I didn't sleep much on the plane and read almost the whole of Karen Blixen's *'Out of Africa'* on the flight. It left my head full of the images and language of Kenya and Kenyan society in the early 1900's, which I figured at the time might not be the best preparation.

I was met at Nairobi's airport by a smiling African driver, holding up a sign, who whisked me away in a large Mercedes through the warm tropical evening. He deposited me at my boss Chris Knocker's house in Karen, the suburb named after the author herself, and where her coffee farm had been situated. Chris lived in a comfortable company house situated conveniently adjacent to the eleventh hole of the Karen golf course. He lived there with Pippa Williams the former wife of another Kenya businessman who seemed to be quite happy to be joining them for drinks. Within the next couple of hours I came to realise that Karen Blixen's book about the 1900's might well be perfect preparation for Kenya in the late sixties as well.

I was told on arrival that we were all going out to a party at Guy and Heather Elkins' house. Guy Elkins also worked at Bensons for Chris. This was about a ten-minute drive away and the party was quite advanced when I arrived, having had almost no sleep for thirty-six hours and a hangover from my farewell party in London. It was all very jolly, there was plenty of drink and the laughter was long and loud. I particularly recall two episodes. A large braying woman was attempting to throw her much smaller husband into the fireplace, filled with blazing logs and parts of her husband. Apparently, he had been dancing too suggestively with his host's wife. Everybody was cheering her on and it was only his obviously experienced evasion tactics that allowed him to escape. In my exhausted state I retreated to sit on the edge of a dining room table in the adjacent dining room. I was surveying the party whilst fighting off sleep when a blonde girl, who had been doing a South African miner's gumboot dance on top of another table, sat down next to me. She was extremely good looking, but I was past caring at that stage. She brandished a cigarette at me indicating that I should light it for her and then came out with

'It's not all elephant hunts and parties you know'.

She snorted, with a touch of derision in her voice, and gave me no chance to answer. I didn't take to her one little bit. She was called Mary Anne Richdale.

Next morning I was driven into downtown Nairobi to meet the S.H.Benson agency and the people who would allegedly be working for me. For a start the receptionist was an extremely beautiful, tall, well-built African lady who quite obviously was respected and desired by every male member of staff regardless of race. Her position was totally secure, and she knew it. Then I was to meet the two art directors, in theory reporting to me. One was a young Englishman a little bit older than I, who was polite enough; the other was Maurice McCrea, a New Zealander in his mid-forties. As far as he was concerned, he didn't report to anyone but himself and set his own priorities. He was actually rather talented so if you just accepted the role reversal you could work well with him.

The other Europeans were an assortment of three or four well-spoken and relaxed account executives of a type I thought I recognised from London agencies in another world. However these were super-relaxed in comparison. Then there was John Bull, the Production Manager, a vastly overweight and overbearing man with a strong East End accent whose wife conveniently was the Finance Manager. Chris Knocker as Managing Director found it more expedient and less taxing to let John Bull actually run the business. Chris had the much more serious task of entertaining on an epic scale. Spectacular and lengthy lunches were a given. Evening drinks also; duck shooting up in the highlands sometimes; a lot of golf; deep sea fishing at Kilifi; trout fishing in the Aberdare Mountains; Rough shooting of guinea fowl and sand grouse down on the Athi Plains stretching away south of Nairobi. It was a damn tough assignment and John Bull made sure that Chris didn't have to pay for any of it.

I just knew I was going to enjoy working at S.H.Benson in Nairobi.

After a night or two at Chris's house I was introduced to my own quarters, a flat in a relatively modern block situated right opposite the fabled Muthaiga Country Club. I had thought ahead on this one and arranged temporary reciprocal rights with Muthaiga through the Hurlingham Club in London to which I belonged. I had also inherited an obliging and elderly African man servant called Kimau who was to cook for me and keep the place clean.

It became evident, sooner than I'd anticipated, that I'd entered into another perfect place that would inexorably drag me into just about complete dependence on alcohol,

The very first bout of binge drinking was on the second night at my new flat, when I sauntered across the road to the Muthaiga Club and, feeling just a bit self-conscious, made my way to what was known in those politically incorrect days as the 'Popsie' Bar, that is the mixed bar, as opposed to the 'Men's' Bar. We all knew our gender-defined place in those days. I stood at the bar nursing a beer and watching, out of the corner of my eye, a quite noisy quartet drinking on the sofas. One of them, a small rather ugly man, said loudly.

'Why are you standing around on your own? Come and join us.'

I was introduced by Peter Shaw, for it was he, to his very pretty wife Anna and Mike Kylie and his wife Madeleine. I was certainly a practised toper, but I wasn't ready for the speed with which they consumed drink. I was told that I should dine with them, and we continued to gallop through the wine, returning after dinner to round after round of whiskies. At around eleven Anna got up to leave and Mike, a tough looking professional white hunter, punched her gently in the stomach at which she sat down again. I started to protest on her behalf when both she and her husband, Peter, told me to shut up and mind my own business. About half an hour later the same scene repeated itself. This time I did get up, pompously slurring some remark about their behaviour, and left. Out in the car park I heard the padding of feet behind me and felt a firm hand on my shoulder.

'You come back and finish your drink right now.'

He didn't have to say,

'If you know what's good for you.'

but that's what he obviously meant. I deigned to go back and finish my drink and a little later managed somehow to stagger back to my flat.

I was woken by the feeling of cold steel on my chest. It was an elderly man applying a stethoscope. Around the bed were my anxious-looking servant Kimau, my boss Chris Knocker and the 'Kiwi' Art Director, Maurice McRea. The elderly man turned out to be the company doctor.

'Wake up, Fitzgerald, its 1975, you weigh nine stone two and you're due for home leave',

were the immortal words with which Maurice greeted my return to consciousness.

Apparently, I had been in an alcoholic coma from which my servant, even by pouring water over me, could not wake me. He had rung the office and told them that the new 'bwana' they had sent him was dead and could someone come and do something about it.

This rather alarming start was put down to 'the altitude', as many such episodes euphemistically were, and was soon forgotten. I settled down to creating ads and commercials with my new team in the laid-back agency in what appeared to be a delightfully laid-back country. Kenya then was under the firm rule of their hero, Jomo Kenyatta and the KANU party, which was basically an extension of the Kikuyu tribe. The other substantial tribe, the Luo, was kept firmly in their place, with the exception of the very brilliant young Minister of Economic Planning, Tom Mboya, who was later to be murdered at the age of 39 in July 1969. He was intelligent, charming and charismatic and had spearheaded the Independence negotiations at the Lancaster House Conferences in 1963. Almost certainly because he was not a member of the Kikuyu tribe and possibly represented a threat to Kenyatta, he was shot, in broad daylight in the busy Government

Road, by a Kikuyu called Nahashon Njoroge. It was a sad loss for the new republic.

The rule of law worked fairly well in those days and people didn't go to ridiculous lengths to protect themselves. Daily life was not visibly corrupt, as it is now, although up at the top there probably was a fair amount of back handing, unfair awarding of contracts and sinecures and land grabbing, none of which might have born too much scrutiny. It felt like a safe and secure society and there was little or no racial tension.

Not long after I arrived, I was offered the opportunity of house-sitting the house in Karen belonging to Lonrho and occupied by Gerald Percy, Lonrho's Chairman in East Africa and Jennifer his South African wife. I leapt at the offer if only to obtain relief from my rather small flat in Muthaiga. It was a beautiful house made famous as the home of Lady Delamere at the time of the 'Delamere murder' when Lord Erroll was shot nearby in 1941. It had been East Africa's most famous murder case and is still not solved to this day, although there are theories. I was to use the roomy and tranquil guest cottage and to ensure that all the Percy's animals and facilities were looked after. It was a disaster. The first to go were the dogs who all contracted biliary (tick fever), I recall that at least two died. Then the horses escaped and one of them broke a leg and had to be shot. I came out one morning to find all the goldfish in the ornamental pond in front of the house were on the surface of the water, white belly up. The PH levels in the swimming pool turned out to be beyond me and the pool had turned pea green. The tennis court developed a sort of mould on the surface. The cook's wife had a most difficult birth accompanied by much screaming and one of the shamba boys (gardeners) had a monumental bust up with one of the askaris (guards) after some drinking and was rushed to hospital.

Gerald arrived back a day earlier than expected and looked in on me on the way up to the main house.

'Come up to the house for a whisky and tell me how it's all gone'. he said cheerfully.

I didn't know where to start. I had killed off most of his household. He took it surprisingly well.

Meanwhile I had settled with ease into the Muthaiga lunch routine and was up in the Men's Bar with Chris when we were assailed by one Count Maurice Coreth. He had been educated at an English public school although his title was Austro-Hungarian.

'Does anybody in here want to go on an elephant shoot with me?', he drawled.

'Fitzgerald will'.

Knocker volunteered.

It took me totally by surprise.

'But I've only just started working for you'.

I spluttered.

'We can live without you. You won't get another opportunity like that'.

The following Saturday morning found me, bright and early, waiting as instructed in the Men's Bar at Muthaiga. I was togged up rather self-consciously in my brand new, still shop-ironed khaki bush shirt with epaulettes, crisp new shorts, long khaki socks and Bata desert boots. Four hours later I was still waiting and lunched at the club, feeling mildly under-dressed. Coreth rang later in the afternoon to tell me that he was still up-country in Subukia. Same instructions were given for Sunday morning. At lunchtime on Sunday, four hours later, Maurice turned up and we lunched. We finally left on the Mombasa Road on Monday morning.

First stop was the row of tin-roofed shops and bars called Mtito Andei about a hundred and fifty miles southeast of Nairobi on the edge of the Tsavo Game Park. We stopped at a very bedraggled looking place that bore absolutely no resemblance to the Muthaiga Club and was called the Mtito Andei *Hoteli & Day & Night Club*, to meet, I assumed by prior arrangement, a Kenyan character called Rusty Mayers who lived in the hills somewhere nearby. He and Maurice exchanged gossip and beers for an hour or two. Maurice was rarely hurried. Eventually we tore ourselves away and drove for an hour or so to a small African village to the south of the main road. Most of the village came running out to greet 'Bwana' Maurice, waving and smiling. Here lived two of his regular trackers who were of the Kamba tribe. We then drove back and, skirting Tsavo, drove for another two hours into the bush bordering the park where the camp had been set up by an advance party on a lorry. This was the sort of camp and safari for which Americans paid thousands of dollars a day, even back then. The sole contribution required of me was a crate of Portuguese rosé wine, known by Maurice as 'stocking wine' because the bottles had a sort of net round them. It wasn't even particularly good wine, and it didn't cost very much either.

In the morning the trackers fairly quickly located a herd of around three hundred elephants with one very old, large-tusked male who was obviously past his best and generally taking up the rear. That was the beast chosen by Maurice. We followed that herd all day through fairly thick bush. At one stage we were completely surrounded by the herd and to my horror Maurice and the African trackers stopped for a chat and a smoke. I pointed in fear to the animals all round us, some as close as fifty yards.

'Don't be daft,'
said Maurice in a normal speaking voice.
'They've known that we 've been with them for the last two hours.'

Eventually the bush cleared and turned into open savannah country. The herd stopped at a water hole and the old male stayed a couple of hundred yards back from the rest. Maurice walked out into the clearing and fired one shot. A brain shot at seventy yards killed the old elephant instantly. It was an impressive piece of hunting of an animal that was fairly certain to be separated from the herd and die that year. In 1969 with millions of elephants running wild in Africa it did not have the same impact as it would have today.

Maurice had a licence for one more elephant on that safari and the trackers had got word of another old bull in a small group of six. The other five were young elephants known as 'askaris' which in Swahili means 'guards'. They were in effect teenagers accompanying the old gang leader. We followed the group for a few hours in the hot midday sun. Then Maurice took his shot which fractionally missed, mortally wounding, but not killing the animal immediately. There followed the most extraordinarily moving behaviour. The other five young elephants gathered round the old boy and, with their shoulders and chests, literally carried him a hundred yards or so. They then propped him up with their backsides and, unaware of where we were, took it in turns to mock charge to all degrees of the compass. Maurice threw me a second gun and, although I was not meant to be part of the hunt, yelled.

'Whenever you get a clear shot, shoot but don't, for God's sake, hit one of the others.'

It took many shots from both of us and at least another thirty minutes for the old bull to be brought down. It was a horrible end to the hunt and after this I was turned off elephant hunting forever. The next generation will no doubt be appalled at the fact that back then we even regarded this as sport. Indisputably it no longer is but looking at the wider context, in 1969 elephants numbered around two to three million in Africa and caused a lot of damage to African farmers. Professional hunters were permitted, at considerable cost, to obtain a licence of I believe one or two elephants per client in a year. The hunting licences paid for anti-poaching units and the whole thing was highly controlled. Now at most 400,000 elephants survive in Africa and the poaching is done on a far greater, and uncontrolled, scale.

Back in Nairobi I embraced the Kenyan lifestyle. Sunday curry lunches, long boozy, lunchtime conversations with highly amusing people on the *'Men's Bar'* veranda at the Muthaiga Club, golf at one of the nine or ten golf clubs around Nairobi, the occasional foray to the Mnarani Club at the coast which was sometimes referred to as Muthaiga-sur-mer.

Looking back now I was a rather impressionable, easily led young man working for an alcoholic boss, several alcoholic colleagues and a more than generous attitude to corporate entertainment.

The good side was that I met up again with Mary Anne, whom I had not taken to on my first night in Kenya. The situation rapidly reversed itself as I now took to her in a big way. We had a lot in common. We were both writers and we both loved to travel. She had come up to Kenya on the back of an American's motor bike two or three years earlier. I had driven up through Africa three years earlier. She had just broken up with her professional hunter boyfriend and she was an extremely good-looking blond and challengingly bright.

I was smitten. The two of us, together with another friend, Brian Macoun, decided to throw a big party for all the people who had made us welcome in Kenya.

We had decided to curry a large eland which would be needed to feed around a hundred guests. We went upcountry to stay with a well-known Kenyan hell-raising young farmer known as 'Shrub' Littlewood and his good friend and neighbour Colin Francome. These two lived up near Rumuruti around a hundred and fifty miles northwest of Nairobi, and ran a large ranch up there, on which elands were regularly seen. M.A., as Mary Anne was universally known, and I set off, following Shrub in my newly acquired Volvo 123, the same as the car that had recently won the East African Safari Rally. The rains had just started and the red murram roads were as slick as ice. I, like most twenty-seven-year-old males, regarded myself as an excellent driver, and I was driving an East African Safari winning car. About three hours into the four-hour journey I skidded violently and turned the car over. M.A. was unhurt but definitely not impressed. Shrub and Colin re-appeared and fell about laughing. It was another 'bloody Pom situation'. They righted the car and we continued on to the ranch. I was obviously traumatised by the whole situation because later that night, tucked up in bed together, I proposed to Mary Anne. At breakfast the next day Shrub and Colin were eager to know when the big day would be. The walls were so thin that they had heard everything. More embarrassment.

Then came the shooting of the eland and the subsequent lifting of this very large animal, not far off the size of a cow, on to the back of the truck. I stood and watched, until M.A. growled "In this country we tote our own meat". I hastily joined in the butchering process lest I give any further offence to the Amazon I was planning to marry.

The party in the Karura Forest outside Nairobi, which now celebrated our engagement, was a huge success and redeemed the situation somewhat. I could not have been happier, even glossing over M.A.'s almost complete lack of culinary skills. Early on in our relationship I stayed overnight, and she gaily offered to cook breakfast only to ask me how to boil an egg. Then one evening I caught her stuffing most of a cauliflower into an electric kettle. Her logic was to her mind impeccable as she knew that a cauliflower had to be cooked in boiling water. Her one speciality dish was known as 'titty rhino', a camp speciality consisting of a fried egg in the middle of a hollowed-out piece of fried bread. I had a lot of those. Actually poor M.A. was blameless because being brought up in a wealthy South African household she had no need even to enter a kitchen. Anyway I was in love with her, and it was blissfully unimportant.

One of our early trips together was, with four or five others, down to the Ngorogoro Crater and then to Lake Manyara. We were due to stay with Ian Douglas-Hamilton, the world-famous authority on elephant behaviour. Packed into one long-wheel based Land Rover, we arrived at the Lake Manyara National Park gates as it was dusk, and we were only allowed to proceed because we were staying with Ian whose house was inside the park boundaries. We had gone a few hundred yards when all the Land Rover lights packed up. It was decided that Bevil Granville and I should sit with torches on the bonnet and guide the driver. We drove slowly round a corner and there in the middle of the road, no more than twenty yards away, was a pride of seven or eight assorted lions. Bevil and I simultaneously leapt for the game viewing hatch, in the roof of the vehicle, almost getting wedged in it, as we both suddenly remembered with complete clarity that the Manyara lions were internationally famous for climbing trees.

My marriage to Mary Anne took place in Johannesburg in September 1969. I flew down a few days earlier and was astonished to find that Mary Anne's parents lived in a very large house with a two-hundred-yard drive and at least ten servants. It turned out that, amongst other things, he was Chairman in South Africa of Hill Samuel, the merchant bank. Before the wedding he took me to one side and spoke

'Look. This idea of working in advertising in Kenya of all places is ludicrous. There's no future in your lifetime for black Africa. Settle your affairs in Kenya and I'll help you invest into an agency in South Africa.'

I was sorely tempted.

'My marriage to your daughter would last approximately thirty seconds if I agreed to that.'

I said,

'She really doesn't want to live in South Africa.'

- under a Nationalist government and apartheid - were the unspoken words.

He grumpily agreed but then said,

'Cancel your honeymoon plans in Kenya.'

Mary Anne's idea was that we were going to drive through the dangerous and almost impassable Northern Frontier District to Marsabit and then go to Garissa, close to Somalia and down to Lamu. I have to admit to a certain frisson of apprehension at the prospect as well, but my fiancée had made her intentions more than clear.

Gordon then outlined his honeymoon plan for us. We were to have a Rolls Royce to drive around South Africa, staying with major South African bankers and industrialists in their private Game Parks, their country estates with private golf course, at his own seaside house in Plettenberg Bay and other unimaginably luxurious destinations.

'Look sir, obviously your daughter has been away from home for quite a while. You may not remember that she is rather determined and will not marry me unless we have the honeymoon as she wants it.'

Gordon had not been crossed like this in quite a while but, in the end, he had to agree. I was quite nervous of him, but I was also quite nervous of my strong-willed wife–to-be and I was in love with her as well. It was a case of a rock and a hard place.

The wedding reception was an exercise in conspicuous expenditure. There were about five hundred people by my reckoning, out of whom I knew my parents, my sister and two others. As the society column in the South African equivalent of Hello Magazine said, "Tout Johannesburg was there!"

On our return to Nairobi we commandeered one of Maurice Coreth's 4-wheel-drive Toyotas, knowing he was in London for a few weeks and leaving a message for him that he probably wasn't going to get until we returned. Our first night was to be at one of the luxury cottages at the Mount Kenya Safari Club which was the only sybaritic element I was allowed by my new bride. The initial plan was to drive the one hundred- and fifty-miles due north straight through from our little house at Wilson Airport. We then did a very stupid thing and stopped for lunch at the Muthaiga Club. Who should be there but Chris Knocker and his lady, Pippa. They announced that, as the Mount Kenya Safari Club cottages had two rooms, both incidentally with sunken Roman baths, they would join us for the first night of our honeymoon as we were paying for the whole cottage anyway. Anywhere else in the world this might have been considered a presumptuous if not offensive suggestion. In Kenya it seemed perfectly reasonable. We set off in convoy together and had an excellent evening.

The first warning blast of the marriage was fired when Mary Anne jumped from the Toyota just north of Isiolo whilst it was travelling at about twenty-five miles per hour. We'd stopped at Isiolo about fifty miles north of the Mount Kenya Safari Club at Nanyuki. We were in blissful mood, and we pulled in at a small shop to buy something that we'd forgotten for the trip. We engaged a young, well-dressed African, who spoke good English, in conversation. Full of goodwill to all mankind we started to exchange contact details and Mary Anne volunteered her Post Box Number in Nairobi. I reminded her jokingly, that, now she was married to me, he should be given my/our box number. Mary Anne disagreed forcefully.

Later in the car, still smarting, I volunteered,

'Maybe we should have separate telephone numbers? Actually, come to think of it we could have two separate houses as well...'

That's when she jumped. That's when I learned that I had married someone who valued her independence more than most.

These days on the fast road that has now been built you can drive the one hundred and sixty miles from Isiolo to Marsabit in around three to four hours assuming, of course, that nobody jumps from the moving vehicle. I recall that in 1969, driving through deep and potholed sand tracks it took around twenty-four hours with an overnight camping stop on the way. The destination was however worth the drive.

Marsabit is an extraordinary, forest-covered extinct volcano jutting out of the desert in Northern Kenya around one hundred and fifty miles from the Ethiopian border. It rises around three thousand feet from the surrounding desert. It was also famous for being the preserve of some of the world's largest elephants, including at the time 'Ahmed', the granddaddy of them all with tusks weighing around one hundred and fifty pounds. Ahmed, then fifty years old, was protected by personal decree from President Kenyatta. Mary Anne and I were to spend nearly an hour in Ahmed's company, watching the old boy at a distance of no more than seventy yards.

The remarkable thing about our stay in Marsabit was the fact that we were the very first people, in nearly a decade, to sign the visitors' book at the camp site next to the crater lake. The mountain had been virtually cut off from tourism since 1960 due to the Shifta uprising by the Somalis who felt it should belong to them. Mary Anne's idea of a honeymoon could best be described as challenging, if not downright foolhardy, as the next stage was to drive through the desert on rough desert tracks to Garissa, in the direction of the peeved Somalis, eventually to reach the more conventional destination of Lamu on the Indian Ocean. I had certainly married someone very special.

The next momentous occasion in our new lives was when our free-wheeling Managing Director, Chris Knocker, smashed his car into the back of an unlit lorry on the Langata Road on the way to an evening wedding celebration. His long-time partner Pippa died in hospital and Chris was so badly injured that he was flown back to England and, even then, was not expected to live. Pippa had been, and I think legally still was, the wife of a prominent Nairobi businessman who had built an aviation business. She had all the attributes of a strong colonial upbringing; good-looking, fearless and headstrong. The story that summed her up best was when acting as a producer's assistant at the making of one of the Tarzan films she showed up the actor playing Tarzan. They were up at Thompson's Falls and the scene called for Tarzan to dive into a pool below the falls. The actor, who could have been Johnny Weissmuller, refused to dive because of his fear of bilharzia. It was pointed out that bilharzia was only contracted by swimming in still water, but the actor remained unconvinced. Pippa grew so impatient that she took off her clothes and dived in herself. She was quite a loss to Kenya's character-filled white community.

Chris Knocker's replacement was a very ineffectual fellow, shipped in from Bensons in Lagos, Nigeria and who had spent all of the war as a London policeman. He wasn't particularly good at understanding the advertising industry and he didn't inspire much confidence in us. He didn't like any of us expatriates either as he quite unreasonably seemed to think that we spent too much time enjoying ourselves, which he quite patently had no intention of doing. He contrived to get me posted to Lagos. I confronted him in his office and ended up walking out and down the corridor to the like-minded Guy Elkins

'Elk, you know we talked about starting a new agency.'
'Yes, what have you in mind?'
he retorted looking up from the three-day old copy of the Times.
'Well, it's just started.'
I said.
'Lunch, I think'
was his eminently predictable reply.

It was a very rash move. We had to leave our company houses within the month and Guy his company car. We were both married; I, very recently indeed and he with two children. We had no substantial savings and no office to go to. All we had were a couple of clients who had always enjoyed lunching with us and who said they'd come along for the ride.

Now my partner Elk was one of the most delightful and amusing of friends but even he would have admitted to being an alcoholic. I had basically gone from working for an alcoholic boss to starting a business with another one. I remained in a state of blissful unawareness.

Any files we could purloin we shoved in the boot of my Volvo which I did happen to own myself. Our first briefing meetings were generally held in the Long Bar of the New Stanley Hotel on some feeble excuse about the office being re-decorated or something. After the client took his leave, I would write some copy and we would get the new Benson's Art Director, who was hidden behind a pillar in the bar and who had no particular love for the new Managing Director either, to run up some visuals on a freelance basis. Guy would devise some marketing and media ideas. A day later we would call the client and meet him again in the Long Bar. It was the sort of service that he had never seen from a regular agency which would normally entail a wait of at least three to four weeks.

One of the hurdles to be overcome was to get recognition as an accredited advertising agency worthy of receiving the fifteen percent commission from the newspapers, and the radio and television stations. That meant having a minimum of ten thousand pounds in the bank. We didn't have one thousand let alone ten. We made an appointment with the general manager of the Kenya Commercial Bank. It had formerly been Grindlays Bank and the elderly Scotsman that we met with was retiring the next month, as part of the only to be expected Africanisation process.

'I wouldn't normally do this,'
he said gravely.
'But I'm retiring next month,'
he continued,
'No other Europeans have started a new company this year and you seem like trustworthy fellows so I'm going to agree to a facility for ten thousand.'

Outside we were overjoyed although Elk later told me that I had asked whether he meant ten thousand Kenya Shillings. Guy had to say excitedly,
'No. Pounds, Fitz, Pounds."
We had an agency.

It wasn't long after this that my new wife announced that she was pregnant, and our cup was running over. Mary Anne also chose this time to enter into partnership with Colin Church and Pat Orr to form a new public relations agency. At the time I remember feeling rather hurt and unreasonably upset that Mary Anne had decided to branch out on her own at the same time that I had taken the risk of starting a new business. I think I had some idea that she should be helping us. On reflection I can only put that down to my own self-absorption.

Mary Anne had set her heart on building a house about ten miles out of Nairobi in Langata on a five-acre plot covered in scrub bush not far from the Nairobi Game Park with a view to the south over the Athi Plains with Mount Kilimanjaro on the skyline, and the Ngong Hills off to the west. Mary Anne's father generously donated the cost of the land which was five thousand pounds and we set about building an A frame house, modelled rather ludicrously on the chalets I remembered from skiing holidays. Our architect, who was a friend, went along with this and turned it into a house we came to love. The plot saw giraffe and warthog come and go on a daily basis and often lion would be seen and even the occasional leopard and python. Mary Anne was deliriously happy.

Whilst the house was being built and Mary Anne grew larger with our first daughter we moved into a row of tin-roofed houses bordering Wilson Airport known fondly as 'Skid Row'. They would not have looked out of place in a Steinbeck novel of the depression in the thirties. They had been built for young bachelor engineers and pilots. They looked as though they could be blown down in the next strong wind and the walls were thin enough to hear most conversations on either side. We absolutely loved living there and that was where our daughter Tara, born on 31$^{st}$ December 1970 was first brought home. As Tara was born on New Year's Eve, I was having a small early celebration at Muthaiga when word came that Mary Anne was going into the hospital. My companions, Guy Elkins and our first client, Ted Darrell of Massey Ferguson volunteered to accompany me. I tried to shake them off, honestly, I did. I rushed up to Mary Anne's hospital room while Guy and Ted found, unknown to me, a cupboard with medical gowns and caps. Both of them wandered through the hospital 'diagnosing' patients they came across. One man was terrified out of his life when Elk whipped up the bedclothes, pointed to the patient's leg and said, "that's going to have to come off". They found their way to Mary Anne's bedside eventually but were then thrown out by security. Despite being nearly as drunk as my friends I didn't actually participate in these pranks but then to my lasting regret I didn't provide much help or support to Mary Anne either and alternated between being overcome with laughter at them and guiltily, and unhelpfully, trying to involve myself in Tara's birth.

It was an exciting and wonderful time but in the back of my mind I remembered guiltily that I had left a child behind in London, who was not with his natural parents, a fact that Mary Anne had been aware of when I married her.

Our chalet on the equator saw some happy times. With the bedrooms downstairs, the upstairs room was in effect just one huge cedar tent with a big plate glass window leading out on to a balcony which had a truly sensational view of the Athi Plains stretching as far as the eye could see with, on a clear day, a view of Mount Kilimanjaro on the horizon. To the right were the Ngong Hills of Karen Blixen and Denys Finch-Hatton fame. They were known to the Maasai as the 'fingers of God' because they looked like the knuckles of a hand, and they said that's where God lifted himself out of the Rift Valley. Our efforts at gardening were rudimentary because we were surrounded by bush and animals. I was sitting with Tara on my knee once when she was insisting on going out to play in the garden. I had to point out that at the time there was a small pride of five lions sitting nonchalantly about twenty yards from the house.

There was a terrible drought year in 1970 and the whole of Kenya suffered. We were woken one morning by the lowing of cattle and looking out saw probably a couple of hundred head of Maasai cattle on what passed for our lawn. There were two Maasai herd boys with spears and before we could stop him our rather overweight and pampered ex-Embassy 'mpishi' cook had rushed out to remonstrate. One of the boys planted a spear in the ground firmly between our man's legs. He ran for his quarters, and we motioned to the herd boys to carry on. They were desperate for grazing.

We used to have our milk delivered in an old whisky bottle from a neighbouring cow by a rather taciturn African on a bicycle. He rarely responded to our good morning 'Jambo' however one morning he ran into the kitchen and asked breathlessly if he could have a cup of 'chai'. We were astonished and for the first time ever engaged him in conversation.

'How are you?'

'Fine'

he answered and went on attempting nonchalance '

'Do you know there's a leopard in your servants' quarters?'

So there I was living in an African paradise and, in just two years from leaving England for the third time, I was now the husband of a rather spectacular wife, the father of a healthy daughter, having built my own house and, with Guy, the founder of our own advertising agency.

What could possibly go wrong?

# Chapter Eight

## LEARNING TO BE A BWANA

Everything seemed to be perfect about free-wheeling Kenya in the early seventies for a young European couple with their own businesses and their own house. Life was for celebration. So we celebrated.

Mary Anne and I had bought an old long-wheel-based Land Rover in which we would make mini safaris down to the Mara, on the Tanzanian border, and elsewhere. We had built stretcher beds in the back and consequently could be pretty self-sufficient. Mary Anne had insisted that we should both get our hunting 'B' license allowing us to shoot plains game which meant anything but the 'Big Five'. We used to shoot impala and 'tommies' (Thompsons Gazelles) both providing delicious meat and the occasional zebra which was turned into a floor covering. The 'B' license was actually quite difficult, and I felt a degree of pride when we both passed. We sat it with a young African who was seeking a career in the Game Department as a ranger. He struggled mightily and we both quite illegally helped him a bit so that he passed. It's to be hoped that he didn't make too many mistakes subsequently as a Game Warden.

Another outstanding safari was to the Nguruman Escarpment on the western side of the Rift Valley down on the Tanzanian border. The Rift Valley runs approximately south to north right through Kenya and is the truly enormous reminder of one of the world's most spectacular geological events. It has created a chain of lakes, both soda salt and fresh water from Natron in the south to Turkana in the north. The view from the six thousand feet Nguruman Escarpment wall down to Lake Natron at two and half thousand feet was enhanced by the looming presence of the Shompole volcano. This particular safari was to get the ideas and photographs for a new tented camp that was being developed by Philip Leakey, the youngest of the Leakey brothers and son of the world-famous palaeontologist couple, Dr Louis and Mary Leakey. The only source of irritation was that Philip never actually paid us. I do remember the thrill of Leakey driving us at over forty miles an hour on the surface of the dried up salt lake with a large herd of zebra and wildebeest charging alongside.

We went on various safaris with friends including one with my old friends the Homershams where we stayed on the newly built island camp at Lake Baringo. Once I water skied across the lake and the driver of the boat thought it would be amusing to slow down and drop me in the middle of a herd of basking hippos in four-foot-deep water. I recall standing in the lake waving my single ski at the hippos who all stood up and glared at me. They are known to be the most prolific killers of humans in Africa.

Another wild adventure master-minded by my intrepid wife was to rescue a high-born Amharic family in Ethiopia from the clutches of the dictator Mengistu. Dereje Deressa was a friend of Mary Anne's and came to Nairobi on a business pretext to ask for her help. Mary Anne and I met the distinguished and handsome Ethiopian in the New Stanley Grill for lunch. We sat at a quiet corner table, and he told us that he and his whole family were in danger of being incarcerated and even killed if they didn't get out of the country. I was put to work on the logistics of the operation whilst Mary Anne and Dereje worked out the timetable and the communication strategy. Dereje was a wealthy man with many business interests in Ethiopia. He was the only distributor of Land Rovers in Ethiopia. They were to communicate by telex, telephone and telegram using code substituting Land Rover spare part descriptions and code numbers for suggested light aircraft landing strips, wind direction and speed. I was delegated to find a plane and pilot as well as organising a landing site and fuel in northern Kenya, to the west of Lake Turkana, then still known as Lake Rudolf.

I got hold of the only possible candidate, a skilled Kenyan pilot called Tony K., fearless to the point of lunacy, who was also to arrange the discreet hire of a twin-engine Cessna. He was not to file a flight plan. Dereje chose a flat, grassy area near Lake Stephanie (now called Lake Chew Bahir) in southern Ethiopia and communicated the coordinates in Land Rover code to Mary Anne. Obviously, the plane and fuel had to be paid for but Tony, typically, refused to take any payment personally as he didn't want to benefit from someone else's misfortune. He did communicate however that at the altitude of the strip the load factor was severely limited and that no more than five adults and two small children could be taken. Tony made it clear that if he saw even one more person on the ground, he would not land to pick them up.

Dereje, who meanwhile was being watched day and night by the secret police organised four Land Rovers packed with people, to drive away from his house in four different directions. The one going south, containing him and his family, was to have a cross painted on the roof. It was a complete four to one gamble and it worked.

I had organised with a pal of mine, Peter Fisher, a Nairobi stockbroker, to drive up to near Lodwar on the west side of Lake Turkana with two barrels of aviation fuel sufficient to get Tony back to Nairobi. Everything in place we waited anxiously for the plane to come in.

To our cheers in the desert air we saw the Cessna flying low over the lake and land in front of us. The plane came to a halt and a furious Tony emerged and strode towards us.

'Come and take a look at the fuel tank.'

He snarled.

We looked in the aperture and saw that there was at most an inch of fuel sloshing about.

'Don't bother to look at the other tank. It's been empty for twenty minutes.'

Apparently a sixth adult had appeared at the strip but Tony, being Tony, had landed anyway and put him in the luggage hold under the fuselage. It had been a terrible risk as they'd only just managed to take off and had consequently used up more fuel than had been allowed for. We got Dereje and his family back to Nairobi and a few weeks later they all travelled to America to settle there permanently. It was just another chapter in my roller-coaster marriage to Mary Anne.

One memorable day the universally respected Jomo Kenyatta, Kenya's first President was to address the nation in Jamhuri Park, a big area just to the north of the city centre. It was decided by a group of us that the 'mzungus' should be seen to be in the audience. About twenty of us, mostly younger white Kenyans, nervously took up a position towards the back of the immense crowd of over a hundred thousand adoring Kikuyus. We got nods of approval from the crowds around us. We think they were saying, indeed we hoped they were saying that it was good that the 'mzungus' were taking part in Kenyan life and respecting their leader. Kenyatta was spellbinding. He talked in Swahili, Kikuyu and English for over two hours sounding uncannily Churchillian by using simple words of no more than two syllables and sentences of five or six words. He would raise the crowd to ecstasy in Swahili then crack a joke as an aside in Kikuyu.

They worshipped him.

Muthaiga Club wasn't really known for its sporting capabilities, but we did, once a year, get up a team from the Men's Bar regulars to play the Nanyuki Club, up north near Mount Kenya. They were mostly farmers, but they were rather more athletic than our Men's Bar team. Guile and careful team selection were the only weapons we had. Our wicket keeper and two slip fielders whose combined weight was almost certainly well in excess of sixty stone, eight hundred and forty pounds, thus heavier than any Lions' Rugby Team front row props. The wicket keeper was a highly anglicised twenty stone Sikh barrister called Sushil Guram. He had long ago abandoned his turban because he was essentially more English than any of us. He had read law at Cambridge, had Half Blues in squash and tennis and a command of English that would put us all to shame. His cries of "Howzat!" were delivered in such a variety of impassioned styles that only the most hard-hearted umpire could resist. To his right at First Slip was Clive Salter QC who weighed in at around twenty-two stone and at Second Slip was Mike Pearson who was of similar weight and girth. The chances of an edged shot getting past these human fortifications were minimal, although they very rarely caught anything. It was quite sufficient that the ball just bounced off them.

I was no bowler, but everybody had to take a turn and in one match, my first three balls were dispatched out of the ground for successive sixes by a lusty young Nanyuki farmer. From the boundary came the languid instruction of our Old Etonian captain

'You've set your trap, Fitzgerald. Now spring it!'

It was at this match that Chris Bates, one of Kenya's leading insurance executives known fondly as 'Master' Bates caused havoc with the members of the Nanyuki Caledonian Society who were having a highland dance meeting with their ladies in another part of the club. We had been celebrating after the match and Chris started rolling the empty beer bottles under the feet of spirited Scotsman as they leapt high in the dance. They were falling like ninepins. They were not amused, and Bates was chased out of the club by the irate Scots. His nickname was changed from the rather clichéd Master Bates to Beer Bottle Bates.

Another attempt at sport was organised by Ulf Aschan, a Swedish tour operator who had deep connections with Kenya and whose godfather had been Karen Blixen's discarded husband, Bror Blixen. Ulf invented the 'Scandihoovian' Games. A team from all the Swedish, Danish, Norwegian, Finnish and Dutch expatriates was to take on the British settlers and expatriates. The events were not modelled on any recognisable athletic events except possibly the tug of war at the end. One of the most exciting races was for a piece of string to be passed down the trousers of the first player and up the trousers, or skirt, if it was a lady, of the next team member. The team that was first to connect all the members, and that could be as many as forty, won the event. All the other events were of this nature. The Games were lubricated by large quantities of Norwegian aquavit (Linie being the best) and were very seriously fought for. At the first games the Norwegian consul was found in a Kikuyu maiden's hut deep in the coffee plantations many days later.

Twice a year there took place the deep-sea fishing competitions down at 'Muthaiga-sur-mer', otherwise known as the Mnarani Club on Kilifi Creek halfway between Mombasa and Malindi. One was the Manchester Cup, presented by the Duke of Manchester. The other was the Delamere Cup presented by the legendary Lady Diana

Delamere. I was down there one year, without Mary Anne as she was away somewhere, and I was told, rather than being asked, that I was to be on Lady D's table at lunch. I was one of six unaccompanied young men at the table, and it felt as though we were chosen as her courtiers. She was an impressive woman alright. One could readily see why she had married three men each one wealthier than the last. Her eyes which were an extraordinarily pale ice blue were her most striking feature. She did not exude a great deal of warmth and I think had only recently had charges dropped for letting a shot gun off at one of her farm managers. I didn't feel it appropriate to engage her in polite conversation about my disastrous attempts to look after her former house for the Percys. The fishing, except for a few very keen diehards seemed to be incidental to the socialising. We would set off at six in the morning and start the day with 'bullshots' which had to be Campbell's beef consommé with vodka. One year they ran out of beef consommé so chicken consommé was substituted which were promptly christened 'cockshots'.

We had a great two-week safari with Leo and Jilly Cooper. Mary Anne was the East African correspondent by then for the Sunday Times and Jilly was coming out to do a big piece on the lighter side of life in Kenya. Mary Anne was asked to take her round the country, and I came along for the ride. Leo's dry anecdotes and Jilly's acute observations were a joy to listen to. We had a hilarious time with them and became good friends. I remember once at The Outspan Hotel in Nyeri the manager, a good-looking young white Kenyan on whom Jilly complimented, in particular and Kenyans in general, for being so fit. "Yes" he replied, "we're the fittest bunch of physical wrecks, possibly in the world". She loved that quote and used it in her article.

Then there was the camel safari we undertook with a party of very 'hoch geboren' (high born) Germans. We were friends in Nairobi with Count Andreas Doenhoff, the man in charge of German aid in East Africa. He had been asked by his aristocratic relatives to organise an original safari in Kenya. He in turn asked us to help and we introduced the person who knew about these things and who had the camels. We were to come along as friends and local 'fixers. The party consisted of mostly late middle-aged and even elderly German aristocrats who all spoke perfect English. In fact on the entire safari of around ten days, out of deference to Mary Anne and me, and out of sheer politeness, we never once heard German spoken within our earshot. It was a fascinating group and we discussed everything as we walked beside our camels (infinitely preferable to riding them) as we traversed the two-hundred-mile semi desert between Isiolo and Loiyangalani on the shores of Lake Turkana. The oldest in the group was a German General and his wife both in their eighties who walked the whole way. He turned out to have been one of Rommel's senior generals in North Africa during the war.

Back in Nairobi Guy and I exchanged our alliances. We started in partnership with Peter Colmore, Nairobi's answer to Noel Coward. He was an incredibly talented and creative man but was not really made for partnerships. He had office space for us and some loyal African staff, but his idea of helping was to appear from his flat above the office at around eleven o'clock in his silk dressing gown and embroidered slippers and spray around a few 'bon mots'. We enjoyed it but felt we had to move forward a little faster. We merged with another agency headed by Denis Cadot and took on as a non-executive director Peter Kibisu who was Assistant Minister of Labour. By happy coincidence he was also the minister in charge of issuing work permits.

The agency would have been much more successful if we had done more than work from nine to twelve thirty. However, the Muthaiga Club beckoned, and the Men's Bar denizens provided the entertainment. The lunches were prodigious, and the conversation flowed. We had incredibly loyal African staff who tolerated all this but one day we arrived back to find our excellent production manager who gloried in the name of Joram Mbogua, seated in Guy's office with his feet up on the desk reading the Daily Nation. He didn't even look up as he said.

'You have been Africanised'.

At the time it was funny, but he was basically telling us that all their jobs hung on us getting and keeping new accounts, which didn't seem too likely in our inebriated state. This was the same African who once uttered the immortal lines.

'Ho hum. Five o'clock. I must go home to teach my dogs to bite Europeans'.

Mary Anne was beginning to get restless and fed up as I enjoyed myself more and more and our marriage was on shaky foundations largely caused by my excessive drinking, even though we had now got a second daughter, Petra. My ever-generous in-laws stepped in by insisting that they would come up and take us out on a hunting safari together so that we could find ourselves again in the peace of the African bush. It was a lovely idea but rather marred by them choosing Liam Lynn, Mary Anne's previous boyfriend, as the professional hunter to organise the safari. Liam and I actually got on quite well, but it was a rather Hemingway-esque situation. I was the only one who was actually going to hunt anything, and the licenses were for two buffalo.

On the first morning Liam, Mary Anne and I went out with trackers and soon came upon a big old bull. We got to within about seventy yards and Liam motioned me to shoot. It dropped to its knees apparently instantly killed with one shot and Liam slapped me on the shoulder in disbelief.

'Great shot! Let's just have a smoke and wait a few minutes. Buffalo can be a bit tricky.'

We walked down to inspect the supposedly fallen buffalo. There was no sign of it. Apparently, I had it hit in the brisket about three inches forward of the heart.

'We're going to have to follow it. This could be a long day.'

We walked for hours and hours with the expert Kamba trackers and after nearly the whole day with the light waning, we came across some Maasai moran (warriors) who told us in Swahili that they would find it at first light and send word to our camp so that we could take up the chase.

After supper, Mary Anne and I went silently to our tent. The atmosphere was heavy with recrimination.

I was woken at five in the morning, whilst it was still dark, by the sound of a Land Rover engine being revved up. I looked over at Mary Anne's camp bed. She had gone.

I guessed immediately what had happened. Liam had decided that I would be more of a liability and had gone to finish off the buffalo on his own. Mary Anne had conspired to go with him to see the denouement. I was livid and found the keys to the second vehicle and drove off trying to follow Liam's expert bush-driving. I was miles behind and arrived to see Liam on the other side of a small ravine firing a single shot at the wounded buffalo in the early dawn light. He killed it instantly. The situation did not help the rapprochement that Mary Anne and I had hoped for.

I was in a deep sulk for the next three days and finally Liam suggested that we go out for the second buffalo. I agreed gracelessly. We were walking through waist high bush when suddenly not more than ten yards in front of us five buffalo, heavily hidden, lifted themselves out of the grass. Liam threw himself down and fired at the nearest male and as he fired, I shot too over his head. The shot missed Liam's head by inches, but it hit the buffalo.

'You lunatic!'

he screamed

'Don't ever shoot behind me again. You nearly took my head off!'
I screamed back,

'It's my effing buffalo! Don't ever shoot first again when we're paying for it.'

Anyway, the buffalo was dead, and I maintain that it was my shot that killed it. It all became rather immaterial, as Liam and I befriended one another and stayed up all night whilst drinking an entire bottle of whisky and playing backgammon. The safari had not done a great deal towards saving my marriage.

My younger brother Jonathan makes me look like an amateur when it comes to addiction to harmful substances. He had made a bit of a mess of his life, and I asked him out to stay in Kenya for a week or so to give him a change of scenery. It wasn't a great time to do it as Mary Anne and I were not getting on, but it seemed necessary. One evening I made the mistake of taking him to Nairobi's one and only casino which was jointly owned by a Kenyan government minister and the mafia. We both had a lot to drink but he rather more than I and he was becoming fighting drunk. I managed to persuade him to leave and as we walked out to the car park, he spotted a bunch of uniformed African soldiers all carrying AK47s. I recognised them instantly as GSU (General Service Unit) the specially formed presidential bodyguard, SAS trained and with a complete licence to kill without any enquiry being mounted afterwards. My dear brother Johnny shouted racial abuse at them, and they started to amble over towards us. The only thing I could do to save our lives was to hit Jonathan very hard and bundle him, half conscious, into the car whilst signalling to the GSU that he was drunk. They laughed and walked away. It could so easily not have been so.

Mary Anne became more and more despairing of my drinking and the late nights and eventually asked for a separation. It was a strange and morose time of my life. I was completely at fault, and I had to leave the house and stay in turn with various friends around Nairobi. Kenya's good at this sort of situation. White Kenya is rather used to it. Not for nothing was there a saying in the colonial service "Are you married, or do you live in Kenya?"

I had a lot of friends and did not lack for company, but I still loved my wife and daughters and felt guilty and miserable. I did not, however, stop drinking. The habit had now become a dependency.

There was one extraordinary interlude when my German friend, Andreas Doenhoff and his wife, seeing my state and suggesting a complete diversion, asked me to accompany them on a trip back to Germany to visit all their very grand relatives in various 'schlosses'. It felt quite unreal to be staying with various Barons, Counts and 'Vons' from Munich to Hamburg to Cologne. I was treated wonderfully and have nothing but affectionate memories of them all. One of my hosts, Count Hermann von Hatzfeldt, who owned at least two villages, was the godson of the German Minister of Finance whom I was actually introduced to at a garden party in Bonn. It was while staying with Hermann von Hatzfeldt in the enormous Schloss Crottorf, in deep forests east of Cologne, that I attended a 'schutzenfest' with everybody dressed apparently in green felt drinking from half gallon jars, eating foot long bratwursts and making impassioned feudal speeches of allegiance to Hermann.

'So sorry about this'

he said in his perfectly accented English,

'I have to go through it every year. It's really quite embarrassing but the village insists.'

I had to go back to face reality in Kenya and rescue of sorts came from Nick Bentley and Tony Thompson who were in Kenya drumming up investment business from white East African farmers. Knowing that I was probably going to have to leave Kenya they asked if I would get involved in a video broadcast scheme for which they had the rights back in England.

It was made clear to me that Mary Anne was going to proceed to divorce and between us we reached an amicable agreement in which Mary Anne was more than generous in not demanding a punishing settlement. I left Guy and the other partners with my share in the advertising agency as it was not exactly flourishing in the nine a.m. to lunchtime office hours' regime. Muthaiga Men's Bar threw a small wake, and I left Kenya much more quietly than I had arrived.

It was heart-wrenching having to leave Kenya, my blameless wife and my two small daughters Tara and Petra. Now I can admit that even at thirty-five years old I was emotionally immature and that the main reason for that, was drinking. They do say that emotional development stops at the age you start to drink alcoholically but that was hardly comforting to my wife and two beautiful children. The whole time could have been so much better spent. The agency could easily have been a great success as Guy, and I were both sufficiently talented and could attract decent clients. We probably would have been able to sell it eventually, as others who came after us did, to a big international agency conglomerate, making enough money to proceed to bigger things. It's not impossible to believe that I might still have been living in that beautiful country to this day. As they say in New York...woulda...coulda....shoulda....

The booze dictated something other.

# Chapter Nine

## DOWN BUT NOT OUT

More than somewhat subdued, I returned to England. The two friends who had approached me in Nairobi about the video idea kept their promise and I moved into an office in Aldwych that housed their investment company. I was the square peg in an office full of financiers and my brief was to establish whether this video idea would work and to set it up as a viable proposition. It's laughable forty years later but at the time video recording was in its infancy and the consortium, which consisted of my two pals, Nick and Tony, plus Lord Cobham as chairman and a mad boffin called Ray Eastland, had contrived a very sketchily thought-out plan to put it to use as an advertising medium.

They had secured the rights to mount screens and show looped video recordings with entertainment and advertising content in all the motorway service station areas in England. It was hardly walking on the moon or splitting the atom, but it actually was an original idea in 1976. Because they were all in finance and knew nothing about marketing, I was tasked with getting it off the ground. I created a name, Sales-on-Sight and set about trying to get video rights to cartoons and newsreels as well as sounding out possible major advertisers. We were making progress but without significant investment, it still remained a good idea on paper only. We needed a million pounds. The boys in the office weren't quite as good as they thought they were at raising the wind, so Tony Thompson and I set about using rather more unorthodox methods.

Tony had been in charge of BAT, the tobacco company, in the Gulf and had a lot of contacts. An interesting story he told me was that one company in Kuwait, I think it was called White Stores, reputedly imported one packet of cigarettes a day for every man, woman and child in the whole Arabian Gulf area. In case you're wondering, the cigarettes turned up at knock-down prices all over Eastern Europe, Western Asia and even Africa. It was basically a smuggling operation on a very big scale and huge money was involved.

Tony and I flew out to Dubai on the cheapest flight possible, spending a night in Damascus on the way, and our first meeting was, rather strangely, in a carpet shop in the souk. Tony assured me that this was quite normal. There were two people in the backroom of this well-stocked carpet emporium, and they were sitting, or rather squatting Arab style on one of the carpets. We were motioned to do likewise and were offered mint tea by the younger man who appeared to be the interpreter. The other, rather more distinguished older man, dressed in Arab djellaba and headdress did not say anything very much and certainly nothing in English. We explained our idea and answered the few questions put to us. The interpreter then said 'the Sheikh would like you to meet him at his bank tomorrow. Here is the address,' handing us a card.

We had only just got round the corner when we started celebrating. This was the big break! We'd done it! That evening we treated ourselves to a lavish dinner and an awful lot of whisky.

The next morning, we turned up hungover, but just about functioning, at the bank. It was an elegant four-story edifice of modern design and looked like a serious place. As we came through the front door into the icily air-conditioned vestibule, a Savile Row-suited Englishman appeared to greet us with outstretched hand.

'Do come in' he drawled,

'You must be Mr. Thompson and Mr. Fitzgerald. The Sheikh is expecting you'.

We were led into what looked like a thousand-square foot office with armchairs, board-room tables and expensive art pieces. The distinguished Arab, whom we recognised from yesterday, now in a suit even better tailored than the Englishman, rose to greet us in perfect English.

'How nice to see you again. Welcome to my humble abode'.

It turned out to be an old Arab ploy. Contrive to meet foreign visitors in Arab dress to see how their manners were and then blindside them in their own milieu. When he had, through the interpreter, said meet him at *his* bank, we hadn't understood that it was actually *his* own, privately owned bank.

He gave us a good hearing, but our hopes were dashed when he said.

'Look, it's an original idea and I understand the appeal, but you've only asked for a million pounds. If you'd started at twenty million pounds, I might have been interested but how can I possibly make anything worthwhile out of an investment of only one million?'

I did try and argue feebly that we could scale the whole project up, but it was too late.

We emerged crestfallen and defeated.

It probably didn't help the cause that I had found in Tony Thompson the most delightful companion but also a most seasoned drinker. He, like me, needed alcohol to enjoy his social life. Yet again I had unerringly got into a partnership with a fellow alcoholic. I feel I can make that judgement now that Tony has very sadly died some ten years later. I was drawn to fellow drinkers because it helped to sidestep any feeling of judgement or guilt.

The next attempt to raise the money was in Germany. Germany at the time was in great danger of deflation as the Deutschmark was far too strong. As a result the government had devised tax incentives to encourage Germans to invest abroad. A friend of ours introduced us to a German lawyer in Cologne who specialised in advising on this. Tony and I turned up in Cologne to be received civilly enough but were told that the initial work would cost us the equivalent of a couple of thousand pounds. He was very authoritative and convincing and so we paid. We never got a single investor from him. He didn't do much to improve the reputation of the legal profession with us.

The Sales on Sight consortium then suggested that we should try and float the idea in South Africa as they were aware that I had good contacts down there. My ex-to-be father-in-law Gordon Richdale was extraordinarily open-minded, kind and generous, given that I was no longer in effect married to his daughter, and invited me down. He was to offer me luxury accommodation, a car and driver and even office space and secretarial help at Hill Samuel. It was an amazing gesture under the circumstances. I linked up with an old friend, Michael Callendar, and we set about trying to persuade Unilever to back the Sales-on-Sight concept in South Africa through their outlets all over the Republic. We came quite close to persuading them but in the end had to give up after about three months and I was forced to return to England. It was the end of Sales-on-Sight and the end of the very modest retainer that I had been paid. Michael took the end of the idea with characteristic good grace. He was an original, always outspoken and capable of acts of complete madness. Like the time he was returning in his car rather drunk and struck a glancing blow to a cow, which happened to be wandering in the road. A policeman stopped him and on walking down to Michael's car rested his hands on the open car windows on the driver's side.

'Take your hands out of my car.'
commanded Michael.

The six-foot five Afrikaner cop gave a slow grin and in his heavily accented Afrikaans accent said.

'Ach, engelsman, you want to be careful talking to me like that.'
'Take your hands out of my car.'
Repeated Michael.

He then pressed the electric button closing the car windows and started to drive off slowly with the cop, red faced with fury, hopping along beside him, trapped like a demented crab. They threw the book at Mike, but it created a terribly funny story for the Inanda Men's Bar

Then there happened the chance that changed my life, but not my lifestyle. I was becoming increasingly desperate in looking for employment with the big advertising agencies in London. For some unaccountable reason they didn't seem to find my CV as alluring as I thought they would. I was going through *Campaign Magazine*, the advertising industry trade magazine, and saw an ad seeking an international media salesman for *Time Magazine*. I have to confess then to a certain amount of snobbery about space salesmen. Hadn't I been a creative director? Had I not owned my own agency? Had I not worked for Young and Rubicam in New York, Chicago and London?

As well as for Bensons in Melbourne, Sydney, Nairobi and London? Was I not a contender? Didn't space salesmen have to pound the pavements and oil up to the agencies? It was only the name of *Time Magazine*, the world's largest selling weekly magazine that made me pick up the phone.

I met with Marc Weinberger, the publisher of Time Atlantic (encompassing Europe, Africa and the Middle East), a charmingly urbane Croatian who had been brought up in Switzerland, as the son of a refugee Croatian banker from Zagreb. He could not have been more agreeable, in perfect if slightly accented English, one of the eight languages he spoke fluently. We got on well enough and he suggested a second meeting a week later when I was offered a job as part of the London sales team of four at a more than respectable salary. He then told me to start work at the sales conference in Cannes at the end of summer. Furthermore the offices were in the Time Life Building in Bond Street, the four of us shared two secretaries, we had bars in our individual offices, there was an excellent dining room on the top floor for entertaining clients, with two butlers, and the expense account was nearly as big as our salaries. It came just in time to rescue me from idleness and provide me with a generous living.

I then proceeded to take lunch even more seriously. I was a regular at Bentleys in Swallow Street. The grill at the Westbury, the Savoy Grill, Scott's, Cecconi's, Morton's, all knew me. Marc put me up as a member of Mark's Club in Charles Street and *Time Magazine* paid the subscription for Sunningdale Golf Club.

My social life was flourishing as I was back in touch with my old friend Chris Knocker and a whole group of people who knew Kenya, loved all forms of sport and were all hardened drinkers. We golfed together, went skiing together, shot together and lunched together. Lunch was often at Bentley's in Swallow Street, famous of course for its oysters, which became for us arguably the most expensive fish and chip shop in London. We were all on expense account and consumed wine as though wine was about to be withdrawn for the rest of our natural lives. Every fifth bottle would usually earn a sixth free and the afternoons would pass in a flash and, more often than not, I would find myself rolling back into the office at four o'clock in the afternoon.

About six months after I joined Time, I was asked, as usual, if I wanted to meet my two colleagues, Robin Leach and Nigel Smith, for a quick lunch at the Westbury. I found them both at our regular table with the *Sunday Times* job section spread out all over the table.

'What on earth are you looking at?'

I questioned.

'A job for you.'

Nigel replied.

'What do you mean? What do you know that I don't?'

'Well, if you carry on the way that you are you'll need to be looking for one.'

Robin added.

'We both like you. We think you could be good at this and we'd rather you stayed. Besides have you got any idea about the sort of bonus that Time pays? I got four month's salary last year for just matching my performance!'

I got the message and eased off at lunch quite a lot. The evenings were however my own.

It has to be said that my two thoughtful colleagues lived well themselves and Nigel Smith in particular was a legend in the whisky distiller community. His body shape consisted of several cannon balls piled one on top of another and he looked like a heart attack waiting to happen. Facially he very closely resembled Queen Victoria's successor, Edward VII, with a naval beard and a forthright manner. He was responsible for the considerable revenue Time Magazine gleaned from the Scotch whisky industry. He drank generous amounts of what he called 'product' and in addition to his position with *Time Magazine* owned a pub somewhere in Essex that stocked every whisky ever distilled. Nigel had an encyclopaedic knowledge of whiskies and was much loved and respected by the heads of the various distilling companies. He was a very good mentor to me but set no great example when it came to cutting back my own intake.

I had my second great stroke of luck at a dinner party at Trish Tallon's, an on-off girl friend who enjoyed drinking as much as I did. At the dinner was an absolutely gorgeous girl called Roseanne Morrison. I drove her home that evening and contrived to see her every evening thereafter. She was fun, she was kind, and she was extremely pretty. She could not be allowed to escape. I proposed to her in the Greenhouse Restaurant behind the Dorchester in October 1978, and we got married at her parents' home village up in Herefordshire in September 1979. I learned later that Trish, who had introduced us, had actually said to Roseanne when hearing of our engagement,

'For God's sake! I didn't mean you to marry him. I was just trying to get rid of him'.

The decree absolute from my marriage with Mary Anne actually came through just the day before our wedding. On with the next.

In the period between the engagement and the wedding Marc had called me in and asked me to be the sales manager of *Time Magazine* in South Africa. I tried to refuse on the grounds that I would rather leave Africa behind me, but he applied pressure and I had to go out to Johannesburg in July 1979, returning for our wedding in September. Later that month, after a honeymoon in Kenya, Roseanne and I started our married life at a cottage in the Inanda Club in Johannesburg.

Life in Johannesburg for a white European with an expatriate contract was as close to perfect as you could get. We rented a large ranch-style house in the still wide-open spaces of Sunninghill Park, just north of Rivonia. We had three or four acres, stables for Roseanne's essential horses, a pool and a tennis court. Add to that membership of the Inanda Club and golf at the very exclusive River Club and my life was complete. The Inanda Club had more than echoes of the Muthaiga Club in Nairobi. It too had a Men's Bar with a collection of affable fellow drinkers. I was welcomed into their midst. It really hadn't taken very long for the after work drinking at the Inanda Club to fall into a recognisable pattern.

I learned much later that our family doctor in Johannesburg had advised Roseanne that I was almost certainly an alcoholic. Out of loyalty she did not share that with me for several years.

I threw myself into the job, the goal of which was to increase the local business of *Time Magazine* and reduce its eighty percent reliance on the huge Rupert tobacco business in Stellenbosch, without, it hardly needs saying, reducing the Rupert business. Rupert then made one cigarette in eight in the free world and was *Time*

*Magazine's* biggest advertiser outside the USA with an expenditure of many millions of dollars. I certainly had to nurture them and visited Stellenbosch or their Cape Town agency on a monthly basis. Once or twice a year when accompanied by *Time Magazine's* publisher I was able to lunch with Dr Anton Rupert the charming and erudite founder of this extraordinarily successful business.

I had come a long way from being the creative writer of the sixties, despising all overt forms of selling, to being quite an effective salesman. As a gross generalisation good salesmen are essentially insecure, are constantly seeking approval and are expert at identifying weaknesses in other peoples' armour, based perhaps on the knowledge of their own. I don't really believe in self-analysis but there's certainly a connection between those traits and heavy drinking. I really became very good at both.

I travelled over the whole of South Africa and loved the challenge. I got good at it and succeeded in doubling the local South African business in the first two years. I earned large bonuses and warm messages from London and New York. Roseanne and I were given a trip to Asia ostensibly to visit the Asian offices of Time in Tokyo, Hong Kong, Taipei and Singapore but in reality, just to say thanks for a good job. I am told by Roseanne that the Peninsula Hotel in Hong Kong was where our daughter Pia was conceived. What a good trip that was.

It was getting easier and easier now to get repeat business for *Time Magazine* as it was an extraordinarily prosperous time in South Africa under the premiership of P.W.Botha. It helped considerably that the price of gold, one of South Africa's biggest earners, in August 1979 when I arrived was around $350 and had gone to over $800 by March 1980. One highlight was meeting Archbishop Desmond Tutu at a small reception that I had to organise for the visiting Chairman of Time Inc, Andrew Heiskell. There were only about twenty people at the reception, possibly because at that time most South Africans would have been quite wary of being seen to attend anything with this extraordinarily courageous man who was the cause of anxiety amongst various Nationalist governments.

*Time Magazine*, which was printed in Johannesburg from one of the earliest satellite links, was the only outside source of news distributed on any scale in South Africa. It was viewed with great suspicion by the Nationalist Government. Accordingly I spent quite a lot of time trying to get agreement for a global supplement in *Time Magazine* extolling the virtues of South Africa. To this end I cultivated the friendship of an Afrikaner government official in Pretoria who at the time was Deputy Minister of Information. He was an affable man and a good conversationalist at the expensive lunches I took him to, in a Pretoria five-star hotel. One day he leant back in his chair after the meal, the brandy essential to all good Afrikaners in his hand and asked in his heavy Afrikaans accent.

'Tell me. Who really owns *Time Magazine*?'

'Well, there are thousands of shareholders which include major institutions and corporate investors. Time Inc. is one of the largest companies on the New York Stock Exchange. I think the Luce family, descendants of one of the founders, now own around two percent. Why do you ask?'

'Come on, Tony (*I hate being called Tony)*'.

He said,

'We have every reason to believe that it's owned by the communist party'.

I was flabbergasted and spent the next hour trying to convince him that in the USA and most of the rest of the world it was regarded as a totally right-wing magazine, if not a capitalist one too. It certainly shone a light on the ruling South African government's view of the world.

We had some great times in South Africa which included a wonderful trip with Peter Read and his sons down into and along the Blyde River Canyon, South Africa's not inconsiderable answer to the Grand Canyon. It was quite an arduous undertaking for two of the Inanda Club's better-known customers. Through Mary Anne I had known Jane Mackenzie well and her father, who was chairman of Standard Bank, had a beautiful private game farm south of the Kruger National Park. We were invited there several times for truly authentic African weekends in the bush. We did game drives and usually saw most of the 'big five' and Ian arranged for the local tribal drummers to come and entertain us round the huge campfire at night.

I travelled extensively in southern Africa and, unsurprisingly, managed to have a good time whilst doing so. Apart from playing golf at the River Club with the great and the good I remember some other notable golf experiences. One was at the Victoria Falls in Rhodesia where I arrived at the Elephant Hills' course to find that the club house no longer existed and the only person there was a small African dressed smartly and completely in white including a white cloth cap and white shoes. He looked like the negative of Gary Player. He emerged from a small building near where the clubhouse had been.

'Are you looking for a game, sah?'

He enquired.

'Well, yes.'.

'I am the caddy master, sah. I will play with you, sah.'

He announced.

It turned out that he was all that was left of the Elephant Hills' Golf Club. The clubhouse burned down when a heat-seeking missile fired by the 'terrs' (as Ian Smith's army referred to them) had missed a small plane flying over the Falls and in the middle of a very full lunch sitting had been attracted by the heat of the kitchen below. The missile went right through the dining room without killing anyone but caused the fire that destroyed the building. The golf course was overgrown but still visible. It had been designed by Gary Player and was one of the longest courses in Africa. It was absolutely heaving with game of all sorts, and we saw herds of buffalo, zebra and impala all over the fairways. The caddy master with his ten handicap and me off twelve at the time, had a superb round which resulted in him winning on the last green. We never saw another human being.

The other memorable game took place in Malawi. I was invited, with a whole gang of Malawian government ministers and senior civil servants, to fly up to northern Malawi for the opening of a new tourist lodge. It was in the middle of nowhere and was in fact not far from where Stanley famously met Dr. Livingstone. I happened to overhear a couple of the African dignitaries talking about golf and I joined in.

'Would you like a game?'

The head of the Malawi Broadcasting Service asked me.

'Well yes, but where?"

I asked.

I accompanied them to a small hut in what appeared to me to be attractive African savannah country with fever trees and waist high grass waving in the warm tropical wind and was issued with rented clubs.

There were four of us playing and eight small boys appeared out of the bush, and we were assigned two caddies each. One to carry the bag and cut the grass with a panga in the area round the ball on the overgrown tee and one to go forward to spot the ball as it landed and cut the grass round it. The 'greens were in fact 'browns', composed of oiled sand providing a perfectly adequate putting surface. Again a cracking and highly competitive game ensued. Apparently the nine-hole course had been cleared back in the twenties by an English District Commissioner when Malawi was under British colonial rule as Nyasaland.

Another great mate, Nigel Twidale, was Marketing Director of the biggest newspaper group in South Africa, which included the shortly to be banned Rand Daily Mail. He organised a wonderful trip to Southwest Africa, which was to become Namibia in 1990. Namibia has only two million people and it is nearly the size of France and Germany combined. It has the second lowest population density in the world after Mongolia and is mostly desert bordered by the wild waves of the Atlantic breaking on the not too cheerfully named Skeleton Coast. It is however a most beautiful desert. We frolicked in the five hundred feet high sand dunes, went seal-watching, shot a kudu for our dinner, examined rock paintings in the desert caves and drank strange beers and liqueurs in the German bars of Swakopmund. Although Southwest Africa had stopped being a German colony back in 1920 it retained a white population that still spoke German at home and their racial views jibed well with the more extreme elements of the Nationalist party in South Africa.

We had a wide circle of friends and Roseanne put together some great lunch and dinner parties where we entertained many of the top businesspeople in the Republic. My former in-laws Gordon and Mary

Richdale continued to shower kindness on us, and Gordon contrived to get me into the most exclusive golf club in South Africa, the River Club, with just one hundred and eighty members, situated twenty minutes from the centre of Johannesburg. They used to say that sixty percent of the South African economy was in the clubhouse over most weekends. As it all seemed to come so easily, I grew bored by the challenge. The after-work drinking at the Inanda Club was now a regular feature. Then Roseanne gave birth to our daughter Pia and happiness reigned. But it wasn't long before I was back in the Club late into the evening.

It wasn't long after Pia was born that I had my first heart attack.

I had been up until three in the morning demolishing a bottle of whisky with a friendly neighbour, the husband of a great friend of Roseanne's. I was due to play in a golf match the next morning with someone I didn't know, teeing off at eight thirty at the River Club. I played nine holes, stopped for a cold drink and basically fell over, to my opponent's great alarm. I was rushed off to the Sandton General Hospital with my pulse rate at over two hundred and irregular. They put me under and rather suddenly woke me up again with thirty thousand volts. However the heart rate was still irregular. I've had to live with that irregular heartbeat ever since as nobody's been able to fix it.

I had been hoping to return triumphantly to England, after my success with Time in South Africa, to be, at the very least, manager of Time's biggest office outside the USA in London or even as Marc's successor as Atlantic Publisher. Nobody else could understand it but I was bored with the job in South Africa. I was tired of the endless dry blue skies of the high veldt in what they called winter, and, despite making some very good personal friends among them, I was put off by the sometimes rather smug and entitled views of many of the English-speaking South Africans, as well as the concealed dislike emanating from the Afrikaners and the resentful oppressed feelings of the Africans. I saw that the American management of Time Magazine was embarrassed by having an office in segregated South Africa but that they were very happy to take the money generated there. I don't suppose I was thinking that deeply at the time but there was something not quite right about the situation.

Roseanne was annoyed with me on several fronts. She was having what she regarded as a perfectly reasonable existence, she had made several good friends, and it was a great place to bring up a child with a marvellous African nursemaid. She was much more upset about my drinking every night at Inanda than I had realised but she couldn't begin to understand why I wanted to get posted away from this idyllic existence. I let Time Magazine know my feelings about my posting after the success I had had over the five years and got a rude shock when I was told that my next posting was to be in Amsterdam to look after the Netherlands and the Nordic countries. I had to accept the decision and got hold of a Dutch lady from the embassy in Pretoria to come to my office two or three times a week to teach me basic Dutch, a language very different from the Afrikaans Dutch spoken in South Africa.

Of course the real reason why Time had posted me to Amsterdam was their concern about my drinking habits. I was blind enough to the problem not to even factor that in.

It was decided that I would go on ahead, find somewhere for us to rent in Holland, and Roseanne would spend a couple of months more in the South African summer closing down our house. I set off in January 1984 for Amsterdam and moved into a service flat in the Singel Hotel, situated on the innermost of Amsterdam's four canals encircling the city centre.

# Chapter Ten

## MARCHING ON WITH TIME

My predecessor at *Time Magazine* in Amsterdam was an Australian, Fergus McLagen, and like most Australians he was affable and friendly and set about willingly familiarising me with *Time Magazine's* key clients in the Netherlands and the Nordic countries. In between I had to find somewhere for our family to live. I would have been happy to look for a house in central Amsterdam but mindful always of the absolute necessity for Roseanne to have horses in her life, I widened the search into what is laughingly called the Dutch countryside. I found what I thought was a fine single-story house on the edge of a small village called Spengen, about thirty minutes' drive from my office in south Amsterdam. It had a field of around two acres and rudimentary stabling. In early spring it looked charming, but I had failed to register that the house and its field were fully twenty feet below the banks of the canal running alongside it. Later on when horses were running around, we noticed that the field started to move. It was quite clearly a floating field. It looked rather rustic and charming in early spring with the daffodils blooming and I naively signed the lease.

Fergus introduced me to leading international players at Philips, KLM, ABN Amro and others. We flew to Stockholm to meet with Ericsson, SAS, Saab, the Swedish banks, and to Denmark for Carlsberg and Jyske Bank. It was all quite exciting and a whole new world for me. One of the first meetings that really stood out was with the advertising director of Ericsson in Stockholm

'How do you find it working for a fascist, right-wing magazine like *Time?*' he enquired calmly.

I was so flabbergasted by his approach that I couldn't really do anything but recount the conversation I'd had with the Afrikaner civil servant in Pretoria who had accused *Time* of being a communist news organ. This caused much Swedish amusement and total disbelief.

In Holland, I was nervously trying out my very basic Dutch language skills on waiters and taxi drivers which one evening I tried extending to a Dutch tram driver.

'Please would you tell me when to get off at Molenstraat,' I asked politely in very bad Dutch.

'Do you think we're all stupid?' he replied in perfect English.

'No, I'm terribly sorry, why would you think that?'

'We all speak at least three languages you know: Dutch, English, German. Some of us speak four,' he added then he went on to ask: 'Why do you want to go to Molenstraat?'

'I'm going to Luigi's Restaurant,' I replied.

'You don't want to go there,' he said. 'Go to Frederico's. It's a much better Italian. Get off at the next stop and take the tram back two stops, and then get on the number forty-nine for three stops.'

'But I'm meeting someone,' I said plaintively.

'Please yourself,' he said rather rudely.

Welcome to the Dutch. They know the answer to just about everything and will not hesitate to put you right. It's not that they don't mean well. They do and they are warm-hearted and well-educated, but they just can't help voicing an opinion. I had my English corrected several times by Dutchmen whilst I lived there. They were invariably right but that made it no less annoying!

Roseanne and two-year-old Pia arrived from Johannesburg in March, and I proudly took them down to see the new house and, as the daffodils were still blooming and it wasn't actually raining at the time, it was received with enthusiastic approval. I then started a round of sales calls all over Holland, Sweden, Finland, Norway and Denmark which meant I was away just about every other week for months. Just as in South Africa I threw myself into the work, and the novelty of the different nationalities really made it interesting. The differences were quite subtle.

The Dutch were shrewd and hard in business and could appear to be ridiculously penny-pinching but by and large we understood each other; the Danes were generally delightful and by far the most laid-back; the Norwegians didn't really have any business for me; the Finns were at times unintelligible with a language that had its roots the other side of the Urals which made it more difficult for them to learn Latin or Germanic based languages; the Danes, Norwegians and Finns were united in their dislike of the Swedes mainly for historical reasons. I got the impression that they thought the Swedes were rather snooty because Sweden still thought of itself as a world power, which it had been for about fifty years in the XVII century when Gustavus Adolfus of the Vasa dynasty was king. At that time Sweden really dominated Eastern Europe, largely with the help of Finnish mercenaries. Apparently Polish mothers, to this day, tell their children to behave or they'll set the Swedes on them. The easy-going Danes had always been enemies of the Swedes and before the Oresund Bridge linking the two countries was built, Swedes who went over to Copenhagen to take advantage of the liberal drinking laws were regarded with some contempt. I saw a bumper sticker on a Copenhagen car that read *'Keep Copenhagen tidy; Drive a Swede to the ferry.'*

Initially it was getting on with the Swedes that really threw me. They mostly spoke near-perfect English, but they definitely did not take to having anything sold to them. In fact the status of salespeople was somewhere between dustbin collection and prostitution. Yet Sweden had an extraordinarily developed industrial infrastructure with the number of world-leading companies totally out of proportion to their eight-and-a-half-million population. There was Volvo, Saab, Ericsson, SAS, Asea, Atlas Copco, Alfa Laval, Sandvik, SKF and a host of other rather esoteric but world-leading companies, and this before Ikea and Hennes & Mauritz were even conceived. It puzzled me how they got to where they were with their dislike of selling. I suppose it meant that they had to make things that were so palpably better that they didn't need actively to sell them. It was a big challenge and particularly as my chief opponent, the sales manager for the same region for *Newsweek*, also based in Amsterdam, was a

Swede. He rather patronisingly took me out to lunch shortly after I arrived and basically told me not to expect to better him in his home market. This was stated in the context of *Time* worldwide having a market share of around 27% against *Newsweek's* 20%. In 1983 in the Netherlands and Scandinavia it was the other way round. This was an interesting challenge.

I remember going into the office of the middle manager in charge of advertising for an Ericsson division and being greeted stiffly, almost sniffily. I tried something new and ostentatiously breathed deeply whilst throwing my arms wide and my head back. This obviously disturbed him.

'Why do you do this?' he enquired, referring to my rather exaggerated gesture.

'I've just flown in from Amsterdam,' I answered, 'and the air you breathe there is quite revolting. London is even worse. It's such a pleasure to breathe clean, pure air.'

He allowed himself a small, very nearly unseen, turning up of a lip that could almost have been interpreted as a smile.

I continued, 'is it true that you can catch salmon off the palace walls in the old town?'

He responded enthusiastically and we talked about the cleanliness of Sweden, the freshness of its ingredients, its probity, its integrity and generally a big Swedish love-in for the next twenty minutes. I had discovered something about which the Swedes were very proud, and it cleared the air in more ways than one.

Actually, the Swedes I knew I got on well with and many opened up to me. It was bit like England in the nineteen fifties in that you were not meant to display any emotion and you generally kept your thoughts and opinions to yourself. I was particularly lucky in that I was friends with a number of Swedes who had lived in Kenya and one in particular. This was Tina Aschan who had been married to Ulf Aschan, of 'Scandihoovian' games in Kenya fame. Her mother had been a Wallenberg, and she was a member of one of Europe's most famous industrial dynasties. Tina lived with her Finnish sculptor husband, Timor Solin, in an exquisite, two-hundred-year-old, three-storey white Swedish clapboard house set amongst old oaks near

Kungsangen, by the side of Lake Malaren, the seventy-five-mile lake that runs from its Baltic Sea entrance at Stockholm. The house was called *Orakers Gard*. Tina and Timor allowed me to stay with them on all my trips to Stockholm (which numbered at least six or seven a year) for around six years. I would hire a car and visit my clients in Stockholm and then return to this beautiful house. I would invariably take a sauna with Timor where we would discuss anything and everything over the regulation bottle of vodka and roll in the snow afterwards, sometimes with the temperature at ten or fifteen degrees below zero.

Meanwhile back in Holland I was trying to get increased business from Philips in Eindhoven. They were amongst Europe's three biggest companies, but they had so many divisions that it was hard to keep up. My main contact, the man in charge of Philips's corporate advertising, was the redoubtable Jan van Haaren. He loved to lunch, and he knew all of us international media people very well. We were a small band of brothers from *Time*, *Newsweek*, *The Economist*, *Business Week*, and the *International Herald Tribune*, all competing for status and market share. Jan played us like von Karajan and the lunches got more and more expensive. It was more the wine that accompanied the lunch. I took him once to a Michelin-star farmhouse restaurant near the Belgian border. The sommelier knew Jan well. In fact they greeted each other like brothers.

'I know this wine list well. Maybe I could find something for us?' he offered.

'Be my guest,' I replied.

He pointed at a Chateau Mouton Rothschild 'Salvador Dali'. Each year the best vintages had labels designed by famous artists. I can't remember the year, but I think it was in the late sixties. I do remember the price. It was around four hundred Dutch Guilders, I think around two hundred pounds in 1985.

'Of course,' I said, 'what a great choice.'

It was the most amazing wine I had tasted to date, but I had to ring my boss Marc Weinberger in London about it the next day. He was surprisingly understanding.

'We've all had the Jan treatment,' he said.

The times I spent in Holland with my little family of Roseanne and Pia were welcome, but by then my drinking was getting out of control. I would down several large whiskies and take out my work frustrations on Roseanne by hectoring and being argumentative. She was the one person I could do that with, and she was pretty miserable about it. When the bad weather arrived the house's position twenty feet below the canal suddenly didn't seem so charming. The field definitely floated. The weather was foul as it always seemed to be raining. The village was downright unfriendly, and Roseanne suffered that in silence. I could always get on a plane to Stockholm, or Copenhagen, or Helsinki; Roseanne was stuck with a small child in an unfriendly and unstimulating environment with a succession of au pairs who, with a couple of exceptions, made for pretty boring company.

We had made a good friend of 'Our Man' in The Hague. He was ostensibly first secretary at the British embassy but was probably doing more interesting things than that position would indicate. He and his wife came to dinner, and he took me aside and told me candidly that I was making a dreadful mistake living in the Dutch countryside and that we should move to The Hague forthwith. It was great advice and Roseanne was delighted. Life in Holland certainly got better, and our social life became much fuller although it has to be said that it largely revolved around other English people in The Hague. I joined Kennemer Golf Club on the North Sea coast, but I did see much more of Roseanne and our house in a smart part of The Hague was very comfortable.

I did however much prefer to be selling in Scandinavia and continued to make a lot of trips up there. I was complaining to my friends Tina and Timor about the difficulty of breaking through when she came up with the idea of a kräftskiva, a crayfish party that marks the end of summer. We set about making it the most memorable crayfish party ever devised. On a hill on Tina's estate was a windmill about a hundred yards from the lake shore. It had a really big open space on the ground floor and the floors above had been converted into a small apartment. It was a truly beautiful old building.

I asked all the great and the good and their partners from Swedish industry and commerce; the top management of Asea, SEB, Atlas Copco, Ericsson, Saab, SAS and Volvo. They were to meet me at the jetty near the Grand Hotel in Stockholm and board a fairly ordinary boat with a canvas awning and a couple of outboard motors. I enlisted someone to pour out unlimited supplies of champagne and I had engaged the services of an accordion player. It was a mild and pleasant evening but within a few minutes there arose distinctly mutinous mutterings from the elegantly dressed Swedes.

'What exactly are we doing on this boat?' one of them asked. 'I have a boat that is considerably bigger and much more comfortable.'

There was a chorus of agreement from all the smart boat owners.

I had to stand up and say: 'Please be patient. This will take about half an hour and then you will be surprised.'

They had no option but to believe me.

As we approached the jetty at Orakers Gard the scene was sublime. The oak trees, the handsome house, the impeccably trimmed lawns, and the flower-filled meadow stretching up to the windmill on the hill were perfect and straight out of one of Ingmar Bergman's more cheerful films. On the jetty in 18th-century costumes was a folk band playing the folk songs of rustic Sweden on authentic instruments.

With the band leading them we strolled up through the wildflowers to the windmill. Over half of the guests were in tears after fifty yards. This was a side of Sweden that I'd never been aware of. They were so moved by the setting and the music that several of the wives came up to me, in tears, and said that we had captured the spirit of a bygone Sweden.

In the windmill we had set up tables for the forty or so guests and served crayfish and aquavit forever. The whole feast had to be accompanied by the singing of well-known Swedish drinking songs. Actually I had arrived with two Americans from *Time Magazine,* and I had told them on pain of death that, when I signalled, we had to start the singing by standing up and bellowing out the most famous drinking song of all 'Helan Går' which means 'Chug it down'. This was met with amazed and uproarious applause from the assembled Swedes. I had arranged for a fleet of cars to start picking up the lifeless bodies from midnight onwards. The party was a huge success judging by the semi-conscious dignitaries being loaded back into the stretch limos. I still think it might have been sheer embarrassment that caused my market share to soar in the ensuing year.

I repeated the crayfish party two years later, on a magnificent 'Tall Ship' in the Stockholm archipelago. It had a crew of around ten and we sailed out towards the Baltic, partying all the way. My daughters, Tara and Petra, came with me to help and I believe they loved it. I remember we organised a swimming race around the boat in which they took part.

The trips to Helsinki were never quite as amusing. The Finns are a strangely silent people and it's hard to read their reactions. I was asked by the Finnish branch of the International Advertising Association to give a talk about international advertising to around two hundred supposedly eager advertising people. It was not a complicated subject, and I was assured by the convener that my audience would understand me in English. I was used to giving a fairly animated presentation and tried to work the audience as usual. There was not a flicker shown for the entire thirty-minute talk. Not a single smile. Not even a cynical titter. At the end I asked if there were any questions. A forest of hands went up as delegate after delegate asked pre-prepared questions read from bits of paper. I wasn't prepared for that and only just escaped with my dignity intact. I was told by my IAA host that they enjoyed it immensely.

I wanted Roseanne to see some of the places I had to visit and on one occasion I took her to Stockholm where we went on one of the huge car ferries overnight to Helsinki through the Aland Islands. We then hired a car and went to visit one of Roseanne's father's friends who had a large estate in the forest to the west of Helsinki. In a tiny hire car we set off through the endless pine forests and drove for hours. As we drove the forest grew darker and the road grew narrower. Disbelievingly we started to notice tanks parked in the forest and without warning about forty soldiers on bicycles suddenly rode straight across the road. This kept happening and we were getting seriously alarmed until we finally found the house in the forest. We learned later at the dinner party (at which the main guest was the

General commanding the Finnish army), that it was the biggest army manoeuvre seen in Finland since the Winter War in 1939. We had driven right through the middle of it.

After that we drove to Tampere and caught a train to Leningrad (now St Petersburg) where we stayed in the famous Astoria Hotel, a relic of czarist Russia, complete with its grumpy old KGB informing women situated on each floor. Crossing the border into the USSR at Vyburg in 1983 was not a heartening experience. The soldiers came into our compartment and motioned us to take down and open our luggage. The smartly dressed officer in charge saw a few copies of *Time Magazine* that I had in my case. He picked them up, glanced at them and then threw them on the floor and pointedly stood on them. Maybe the guy at Ericsson was right after all in his assessment of Time as a right wing, fascist magazine! I don't hold with that view.

We were, like anybody who had ever visited them, stunned by the Hermitage and the Summer Palace. Our guide in Leningrad was a charming, good looking twenty-five-year-old man who spoke near faultless English and spirited us to the front of every queue including the three-hundred-yard line-up to get into the Hermitage itself. After a day or two we felt that we got on well enough to ask him

'Why do you do this job? You seem to be very well-educated. You speak such good English, and you seem to know a huge amount.'

His answer was amusing.

'I have a master's degree in Bahasa Indonesia, the Indonesian language. I was being prepared for a major assignment at the Russian embassy in Djakarta. When Suharto was no longer in power, they no longer wanted to deal with the USSR. Now the USSR has no further need of me.'

On a trip to Stockholm I was travelling with Strobe Talbott who was then one of *Time Magazine's* leading journalists. His particular area of expertise covered the disarmament talks between the USA and the USSR. He was already the author of several books. As we discussed the next day's programme he casually interrupted with,

'Fix up a meeting with Olof Palme before we leave, will you.'

'But he's the Prime Minister,' I nervously replied.

'Yeah, and he loves journalists, and he loves publicity. He'll see us.'

I had never undertaken anything so presumptuous, but I found the number of the Prime Minister's office and spoke apprehensively to his private secretary.

'Strobe Talbott of *Time Magazine* is in town. Could Mr. Palme spare a few minutes?'

'But of course, when would you like to come and see him?'

Nine o'clock the next morning saw Strobe and I sitting in the Swedish Prime Minister's office, Strobe with his feet up on the small coffee-table in front of him. I was in an armchair facing Palme. They obviously knew each other quite well and the conversation was relaxed and informal. I added nothing in case I disturbed the flow of Strobe's questions. I became aware of Palme staring at me and as I looked up, I realised he was trying to outstare me and make me drop my eyes. God knows why. I found myself feeling almost angry and stared fixedly back and he suddenly threw his head back and laughed. To this day I can't imagine what he was playing at. Strobe went on to become Deputy Secretary of State under President Clinton.

It was only two years later in February 1986 that Palme was murdered in the street, and they never caught the man who killed him. It was a strange feeling to hear of the murder of a man whose hand I had shaken and spent over an hour with. I had been mildly irritated by the events of the meeting, but he was a world figure, immensely intelligent and extremely controversial. I was proud to have spent some time with him, even as a very secondary figure in the meeting.

In Den Haag once I chanced to have a short conversation at a news-conference drinks' party with the much-admired Dutch Prime Minister, Ruud Lubbers. He was an easy-going, charming man who created consensus governments and was the longest serving Prime Minister of Holland. He was in complete contrast to the polarising, left-wing, anti-American Palme.

It was around about then that the unpredictable and, at times, irrational, *Time Magazine* management struck. My Dutch salesman Aysso Reudink and I had managed to reverse the market share situation with *Newsweek* and *Time* was back in its rightful place. So, naturally, they decided to close the office. I had to fire the Dutch salesman immediately, which was extremely painful and totally unnecessary. I took a long time to convince him that it was absolutely nothing to do with me as I both liked him and thought a lot of his selling skills. I was told to come back to London to be re-assigned to a sort of roving job covering all the parts of the world that nobody else wanted to cover. I was to continue with the Nordic region but was to add the Middle East and the still communist Eastern Europe.

Luckily the knee-jerk American who thought all this up was replaced as publisher by my good friend, Alain Ranchoux, who had managed Paris successfully. He asked me to be in charge of all sales strategy and long-term business development for the whole of Europe, Middle East and Africa and to try and work with the other Time Warner divisions such as CNN, HBO, Warner Music and all the other magazines. On the face of it the role sounded pretty exciting but then it turned out that the activities proposed had to generate their own budget in their entirety.

Shortly before this new role was devised, and not long after my office had been closed down, I was informed that I had, after my Scandinavian exploits, been awarded the Time Inc. President's Prize for *Time Magazine International*. Their sense of timing was immaculate. It's a source of bewilderment and amusement as to how alcohol addiction affects people in different ways. There I was, by now reliant on alcohol both as a reward, and as a way of masking anger and fear, being able to function well enough to get a 'world's best' award within what was then one of the world's largest media companies.

I was flown to New York to meet and have several meals with all the top people in Time Inc. This was in the company of five others who represented *Time USA*, *Fortune*, *People*, *Sports Illustrated* and *Money*. We were treated like royalty for four days and when we first met up in the Time Inc hotel, Charlie Thomas, one of the other recipients whispered to me:

'I'd guess that there'll be a cash award for this as well. Do you have any idea what it will be?'

Now, I was a good decade older than the others and was a decade or so more cynical.

'There'll be no cash. Getting recognition from the gods is the award!'

He gasped. 'You've got to be kidding. I bet you ten bucks we get something'.

'You're on,' I replied.

Sure enough, right at the end of our stay, we gathered for the presentation of an extremely expensive and extremely odd trophy in the shape of a crystal pyramid designed by Cartier, and costing I would guess at a thousand dollars. I felt a hand at my side shoving something into my pocket. It was Charlie paying me ten bucks with a disgusted look on his face.

Charlie and I went out that evening on our own to P.J. Clark's hamburger joint and well-known bar. Typically, I drank about six large whiskies at a steady pace. In the same time he consumed three cold Budweisers, He was very preppy and very earnest.

'Do you always drink as much as that? he enquired.

'What on earth are you talking about?' I said.

Time Inc was a major sponsor of the Olympic Games, and they had a large cruise ship in Barcelona harbour for the duration. We, with our wives, were to be on board to act as hosts for around six-hundred guests. We changed over every four days, and I was required for two hosting periods. It was an incredible time as we had the best seats to everything and partied loud and long into the night to the strains of a sixteen-man Californian rock band playing almost non-stop on the bridge. Also in 1992 were the Winter Olympics when *Time* took over a large hotel in Courchevel. The French skiing public had decided not to come because of anticipated over-crowding. The result was that the Time Inc. party of around four hundred had the mountains to itself and we were allocated a guide to every five or six guests. These were the sort of occasions when it was really worthwhile working for Time Inc despite all its political machinations and Machiavellian plots.

Just after the Olympics I was delegated to go to a cocktail party in Belgrave Square for the major backers of the Paralympic Games. I was asked to represent *Time Magazine*. Diana, Princess of Wales was the United Kingdom patron of the Paralympics and was of course the guest of honour. I was talking to the Olympic gold medallist from

Moscow, Duncan Goodhew, with whom I had become friendly in Barcelona He suddenly grabbed me and pushed me forward towards Diana.

'Here's the man with all the money, Your Highness,' he said.

She turned and gave me a thousand-watt smile.

'I'm afraid I'm not the one who makes those decisions, Your Highness!' I stammered.

In high heels she appeared to be every bit as tall as I was at six-foot-two. Her handshake was as firm as a man's and her charm and looks were genuinely overwhelming. She used her cornflower blue eyes expressively and to great effect often by looking out from under the lashes. Her smile was kindly and without artifice.

We engaged in conversation on our own for nearly fifteen minutes. It probably couldn't be described as a momentous conversation and was mostly about the Olympics and what *Time Magazine* hoped to achieve by being involved. I may not remember the words we exchanged but I did feel that she was genuinely interested in me as a person and concentrated hard on the answers I gave. She had an almost flirtatious way of communicating which had little to do with me I am sure, but was just the way she communicated. It had to do with being pleasing and helping somebody else out in case they found it difficult to talk to her. In fact, she was so expert at putting me at my ease that the thought flitted through my mind that I could very nearly ask her out to dinner. Sadly I didn't.

Part of my role at *Time* was to visit the rather more far-flung parts of the Atlantic area. I went to the Middle East many times and visited Dubai extensively in the mid- and late eighties when it was still possible to distinguish its character as an old Arab port. There was a certain charm to it then although the skyscrapers were beginning to proliferate, and the first two golf courses had just been built. The main clients there were Emirates Airlines and the Dubai Duty Free operation which was already growing at a meteoric rate. Like most of the duty-free shops it was run by Irish executives, as the very first duty-free operation had been invented at Shannon Airport to catch American travellers landing there on their way into Europe back in

1947. They developed an expertise that was sold on to countries all over the world and it didn't entirely hurt that I had an Irish name.

I was once asked to go to Lebanon by an advertising agency owned by some Christian Lebanese at round about the time that Terry Waite, the Church of England cleric, was kidnapped. The idea was that *Time Magazine* might put together a sponsored supplement that portrayed Lebanon in a positive light. I told the people who made contact that I could only go if they fixed the visa and that they guaranteed to meet me actually at the steps as I came off the plane. This they did in the latest model Jaguar which was unexpected. There were three Lebanese in the car. All of them wearing impenetrable dark glasses and sporting fawn camel-hair coats thrown casually over the shoulder in requisite Mediterranean style. They spoke French amongst themselves and that was the only thing that stopped me thinking of the mafia.

After the initial introductions one of them said, 'I'm afraid that sight-seeing is limited due to the war. We'll take you to the last remaining sight.'

They then drove the Jaguar very carefully down the potholed road that marked the Green Line. This was where Christians and Arabs had confronted each other over the past ten years. It was a horrific sight. For about a hundred yards on either side the buildings had all but disappeared. Then there were buildings with the fronts blown off displaying the wrecked lives of thousands of Lebanese. They had made their point very effectively.

The head of the Lebanese ad agency told me a sobering story about his son who was arrested and charged with a serious crime. He was found guilty by the court but the father, my contact, suggested that the judge, before passing sentence, should look out of the window where he saw a small army of Christian militia armed with automatic rifles. The son was released. This is how Lebanon operated in those times.

Payment was always a problem. I was in Jeddah seeing the Lebanese-owned agency for Saudi Airlines. Before I was able to get any more business from them, I was instructed to get them to pay the two-million dollars plus that they had owed Time Inc. for a year. The agency swore that the client had not paid them. I took a taxi across town and visited the client who swore that they had paid the agency. I was incensed and determined to get action. I took a cab back to the agency and confronted them again. I think I made a total of four taxi rides that day and with threats and cajoling managed to get a million dollars paid. I will never know the end of that saga as I think *Time* eventually refused to take any more business from them.

I managed to travel to a lot of contrasting places at *Time's* expense: Malta, Poland, Hungary, Bulgaria and even Father Christmas's town Rovaniemi in northern Finland, and Iceland. I will never forget driving on my own out to Thingvellir in Iceland, the bleak and desolate site of the world's first recorded democratic parliament in 930 AD. It is on the mid-Atlantic ridge which is designated by a cliff maybe one-hundred-and-fifty feet in height that runs, north to south, along the entire length of Iceland. The story imparted was that each of one hundred Icelandic males voted for a representative to decide whether they would follow the old Norse gods or embrace Christianity. Christianity won by a single vote and all parliaments subsequently were modelled on this. With the wind howling and the grey clouds scudding over the bleak, volcanic landscape it was indeed a haunted place.

I had occasion to visit Israel a couple of times and *Time* had a rep there who was a South African Israeli and who was well connected with the military and the politicians. He did not produce any business but, as he constantly reminded us, he was well connected. On my first visit he threw a drinks' party to which came about fifty of his good connections. Men and women spent the entire time shouting and gesticulating at each other and at one stage I thought physical fights were about to break out. When they'd all left, I asked our man how he thought it had gone. He told me that they had all enjoyed it immensely and that Israelis were never happier than when they were arguing with each other.

To visit Israel and other countries in the Middle East required two passports and a return to the next country on the itinerary via Cyprus. I stopped off for a weekend once and stayed in the Troodos Mountains to try and get some skiing. The top of Mount Olympus is actually nearly two-thousand metres, so the snow is usually good enough. I stayed in a surprisingly large and old-fashioned hotel and on the first evening the manager, who turned out to be the owner, joined me and said he would take me skiing the next morning. It really wasn't at all bad and he was a superb skier. I asked him how he came to be so good.

'I was at Oxford University, and I was captain of the Cyprus ski team at the Olympics was his reply.

'How did you do?' I asked, possibly rather patronisingly.

'Not brilliantly,' he replied, 'but we did beat all the British skiers.'

The skiing trip led to a glorious confrontation with a Jordanian Customs official. He took my ski boots out of the case and enquired, 'What are these?'

'Ski boots' I replied helpfully.

He thought for a couple of minutes.

'No snow in Jordan,' he said suspiciously.

When visiting Malta I decided to try and contact the famous Dame Mabel Strickland who was a distant cousin. My mother's maiden name was Strickland. Mabel Strickland, who was unmarried, was the only daughter of the last British Prime Minister of Malta, Lord Strickland, and was particularly famous as the owner of the *Times of Malta* which vehemently opposed everything enacted by the current, rather despotic ruler of Malta, Dom Mintoff. There was mutual loathing on both sides and one day Mintoff's thugs burned down the building housing the newspaper. Dame Mabel had hidden a spare printing press in a farm building and the *Times of Malta* appeared with its patent oppositional bias as usual the next morning. Made you proud to be British!

I was permitted an audience with Dame Mabel and was led into the drawing room where she was holding court. There were two admirals in the room, one American and one British. They were perched on the edges of their armchairs and looked like frightened rabbits as this formidable woman harangued them about something that I didn't get to understand. I don't think she had any idea who I was but just motioned me to sit down and be quiet.

Actually I came close to killing Dom Mintoff myself. I was playing golf with a very agreeable Englishman who had a business in Malta.

The golf course was situated in the middle of the Valetta Racecourse which completely encircled it. I had not been playing particularly well and was hooking the ball to the left, with great force. As we approached the last tee my partner said quietly 'Would you mind not hitting a shot just yet. The three men on horseback approaching us are Dom Mintoff and two of his bodyguards.' As they passed us, we doffed our caps. He was after all Head of State. I took my shot and hooked my ball violently to the very spot where Mintoff had been.

'Blast!' said my partner. 'If I'd known you were going to be so accurate, I'd have made you take the shot!'

Mintoff was not a popular leader.

Then in London there appeared, as publisher of *Time Atlantic*, the ambitious son of a Greek millionaire ship owner. He had remarkably little personal charm and no great selling skill, but he had completely mastered the art of the politics that accompanies a large American company. We neither of us liked each other but he was, for a short time, my boss. The only perceptive thing he did for me was to suggest that I speak to somebody about my drinking and recommend me to an absolutely charming lady who suggested that I check in for six weeks for a course paid for by Time Inc. She made it sound like the offer of a villa in Mustique. I declined and told her and the Greek that I could stop drinking anytime I liked. I did just that for three months but then chanced a few pints of beer, a couple of glasses of wine and within two weeks was back at the same level. I still don't like the Greek, but he did have the intelligence to see that I needed help way before I sought it for real.

Right on cue, after giving me the President's Prize, it was about a year and a half later that *Time Magazine* dismissed me. They paid me a large enough cheque and left me with, at the time, a decent pension. It was done in a dignified way, but I was hurt by the whole process as I had assumed from the previous year that they had thought a great deal of me. It didn't help that I wasn't American and there were people around in the company who suspected that I drank too much. I have to face up to the fact that had I not drunk so heavily throughout my charmed career I might have done considerably better.

It was about this time that I was playing cricket up near Watership Down, of rabbit fame, with a bunch of middle-aged South Africans and Englishmen who had lived in South Africa. It was a regular annual fixture and was not taken even remotely seriously. Drink was abundant and excessive athleticism was generally greeted with mocking jeers. I was bowling, not my strong point, and was hit for successive sixes which irritated me somewhat. I lengthened my stride from three paces to five and the batsman swinging lustily again was caught in the outfield. As the captain grudgingly congratulated me, I felt a tightening band round my chest and my forehead was beaded in a cold sweat. I went out slowly to field on the boundary and then stupidly ran for a hard-hit ball. I felt dreadful and staggered off the pitch to sit down. One of my friends remarked on my colour and asked me for my doctor's number. I spoke to my doctor on the phone for no more than thirty seconds and he remarked calmly over the phone 'you've just had a heart attack. Ring for an ambulance'. In less than twenty minutes an ambulance arrived, and I was shoved on a trolley and given something under my tongue that revived me.

As I was wheeled off, I heard our captain: 'I don't want any unnecessary displays of emotion. A small round of applause will suffice.'

I was laughing so much that I nearly fell off the gurney.

Then a voice cried out: 'Fitz, may I have your ploughman's lunch?'

I laughed all the way to the hospital.

# Chapter Eleven

## HOW DID I GET HERE FROM THERE?

I couldn't quite believe it. My nice comfortable career seemed to be over. I didn't exactly have a nervous breakdown about it because I was still drinking steadily and anaesthetically in the company of like-minded people, and I had a decent payoff that left me with a false feeling of security.

What to do next? I did try and find roles with other media organisations but at the age of 54 I discovered that having got on the short list the positions were usually filled by people twenty years younger. Times were starting to change. Maybe the best way to sell and manage sales were no longer fuelled by expensive lunches and alcoholic friendships. I soon discovered that they weren't.

I'm a bit hazy now as to how I lurched into the next part of my career but, through a former Time Magazine contact who understood my way of selling, I found myself representing MIT's Technology Review on commission. Coming from MIT it was immensely prestigious but on its own gave me no chance of getting close to my previous income.

I then had the luck to fall in with an old friend, Basil Bicknell, who had just retired as international advertising director of the New York Times. The joke in the industry was that Basil was the only person ever to have achieved honourable retirement from any international publication. The rest were either fired or died of drink. He was a wonderfully kind and well-connected man. He was one of the few men left who cultivated a monocle and in conversation would claim to either know intimately or be related to just about everybody one had ever heard of. He certainly knew everybody in our media world, and he was known by important figures from Korea to Argentina, from New York to Paris. He did all this without apparently ever having a clue as to how to read a rate card. He used to lunch with the chairman of the target company and announce that 'his man' would contact 'your man' to thrash out the details. He had done favours for so many people that they all loved him and gave him business.

I was still obsessively hard-working despite being largely fuelled by whisky. Actually I now know that my manic work habits were probably another symptom of addiction. I used both to avoid meeting up with myself and the obligations to my family.

With Basil's contacts and my non-stop work we managed to get some more American media companies on board and then ambitiously set out to cover the whole of Europe.

That was never going to work and, after one crowded fortnight in Switzerland when Basil and I visited almost every Swiss watch manufacturer in the Jura Mountains and Geneva, we came to the conclusion that we couldn't possibly cover the whole of Europe as we had originally intended. We set up a network of people in France, Germany, Spain and Italy who had worked in international media. The proposal was that we would get and manage the contracts with the Americans, and they would sell in their own country. We would get a share of the commission earned by them and we ourselves would sell in the British Isles.

The final part of the puzzle, namely finding an office, was solved by meeting David Wright who had been a Group Head at the Sunday Times, and who had offices in Battersea. He and his wife Jane had quite a healthy business representing a successful trade magazine. We undertook to introduce him to the world of international media and split the profits. It was a relationship that was to last over ten years.

Whilst working in Battersea I was still spending two or three nights in London and many of my evenings in the Phene Arms pub in Chelsea occasionally drinking with, George Best. I was in the Phene more often than George who used to pop in two or three times a week. He used to arrive, always smiling, with two or three companions which sometimes included his attractive blond wife. He was smaller than I had imagined, and his good looks were still evident although, understandably, a bit raddled by drink. We knew that he came there because it was a pub that was very much for people who were there to drink seriously and not bother celebrities. We treated him politely, exchanging pleasantries occasionally. He was always well-behaved and when he'd had too much, one of his mates, or his wife, would gently lead him out. It was so sad that he could never beat alcoholism. He had been a genius and seemed to our possibly clouded judgement a genuinely agreeable figure.

After about four years of this life, Roseanne and I were at a New Year's Day lunch given by friends living about six or seven miles away. She decided to go home in a separate car at around six in the evening. It was at around ten pm that my friends suggested that I would be better off staying the night and returning to my family the next morning. I rang Roseanne who appeared to accept this idea, albeit rather more frostily than usual.

In the morning I drove into the driveway to find Roseanne and my thirteen-year-old daughter Pia loading the pony into a horse box. The other half of the horsebox seemed to be full of luggage. I enquired gaily, where they were off to. Pia said nothing. Roseanne just said.

"We're leaving. I'm bored with this,"

I tried to get more of an explanation from them but that was it. After another twenty minutes of packing they left in total silence with all their belongings and the pony. I was completely bewildered. Had I not done the responsible thing and stayed the night rather than drive? Wasn't I now completely sober? I had absolutely no idea where they had gone. I had absolutely no idea what to do next.

Then, mercifully, my eldest daughter Tara turned up and after three days wrangling persuaded me to see my local GP. Everything moved quickly after that.

This is where this book started. My strong-minded wife finally had had enough and, by leaving as abruptly as she did, probably allowed me to live a fulfilling life for another 25 years and counting!

After four weeks in the Priory I nervously started to go to AA meetings. Initially I went to two or three a week which is rather less than recommended. I started to listen more keenly to what others were saying. During my third or fourth meeting in our small town I ventured to respond to a 'share' with a few words endorsing what the previous speaker had just said. Afterwards, whilst we were having the compulsory instant coffee and fag outside the meeting, one of the others shambled up to me. He was a skinhead welder from Reading with an almost unintelligible rural Berkshire accent. "I liked what you said" he stated. Now this man was in AA because he was riven with guilt for repeatedly beating up his wife when drunk. He found it difficult to look you straight in the face and he had been in prison. You would not buy a used car from this man. In fact you'd probably do everything to avoid him. In the course of the next year of meetings he became a good friend. He was able to say, in his own way, some of the wisest things I've ever heard anyone say about human weakness. He was deep-down a good man blighted by the serious illness of addiction. He kept coming to the meetings and he got stronger and stronger. I do so hope that he is still in recovery because he deserves to be.

I used to go to meetings in St Peter's Church in Eaton Square when I was in London. That was really something else but served exactly the same purpose. They were much bigger with up to a hundred and fifty people. They were a very different group of drunks. Smart executives and professionals, male and female, were the norm. There was always a large representation of smartly dressed American women who terrified us all by being so articulate when they shared their experiences. They could sometimes make the rest of us all feel very inadequate.

After a year or so I felt that I should really do something to show Roseanne and Pia how much I welcomed them back in my life, so I took them to New York and then to skiing in Vail as a sort of penitential holiday. As a well-remembered shared experience I felt it was a great success. We stayed with good friends in Manhattan and Pia and Roseanne did much shopping. A highlight was accompanying Pia down her first double black diamond ski run in Vail. That's a good memory because she has now become a really strong and graceful skier and loves it as much as I do.

I went to an AA meeting in a little logging town about ten miles down the valley from Vail. I needed to get away from the fashionable, be-furred New Yorker drunks that would almost certainly constitute the attendance at the Vail meetings. This was just an ordinary little Colorado town. The people there were exactly the same as in my little town. They even said exactly the same things in their 'shares'. It was comforting to discover the universality of the solution to this illness.

My colleagues and friends in our little business, Basil, David and his wife, Jane and Jon were incredibly understanding and supportive, but something was still unresolved. I could not hope that my family would rush to forgive me, but we were slowly moving in that direction. The circle needed closing.

Out of the blue I received a card in an envelope. It had a quote about families from F. Scott Fitzgerald on the front. It read:

*'Hi, I'm looking for my father. If you knew Shari S\*\*\* in Chelsea in the sixties you may well be him. If this rings a bell give me a call (mobile number). If not, I'm sorry to have spoilt your breakfast and feel free to bin this card."*

I had two reactions. Obviously, one was shock that after thirty-seven years, my 'Chelsea' son named by us Simon, now called James, had tracked me down. The other was a slow grin at the humorous way he had expressed it.

When we met up at my club in London, I liked James as soon as I saw him walk across the room. I recognised immediately the likeness to his mother. We talked for nearly three hours at lunch. He had been trying to track me down for nearly twenty years but had been unable to do so because I had moved from continent to continent since his birth. He had only been able to find me through an entry for my limited company and sent the card as a complete long shot.

He was likeable, sane, intelligent, successful and apparently forgiving. He is a successful and happily married barrister with two intelligent, well-made and talented sons. I have seen him and his wife and sons many times since and enjoyed every encounter. I have absolutely no right to feel proud of him, as I had absolutely nothing to do with his upbringing, but I unashamedly do. It was in a sense the final piece in the jigsaw of my recovery.

The conversation with the psychiatrist twenty years earlier was where I came in and that was the start of the most productive journey of any that I had ever made. Apart from the odd holiday and business trip, and one memorable trip to Indonesia and Vietnam with Roseanne, and another to Australia, I have not really moved out of London and the south-east of England during the past twenty years, but it could be said that I travelled further in that time than I had ever thought possible.

So how did I stay alive after the punishment I inflicted on my body and mind in five continents over a period of nearly forty years? Twenty years ago I was on course for a premature death. I had given myself two heart attacks, I had a permanent irregular heartbeat and I had earned myself type two diabetes caused by a body weight of around eighteen stone (two hundred and fifty pounds). My second wife had walked out on me for the same reason as the first. My three daughters, so beautiful, so bright, and of whom I was so proud, found it difficult to relate to me. I was unpredictable with them so I cannot blame them. I think it is probably true to say that most of my closer friends and acquaintances were heavy drinkers and that most of my drinking friends in Kenya had died in their late fifties and sixties. Quite a few friends in London were risking the same fate and so was I.

It sounds counter intuitive, but one of the problems that I later identified, was that I had an incredibly strong head for alcohol. I could drink for days and never fall over. I may have talked garbled rubbish, and I picked an awful lot of arguments, but I never fell over. I sometimes think that if I had been more susceptible, I would have acted earlier and saved people (who didn't deserve it) an awful lot of heartache. All I could think of was the fun and all we sought was the camaraderie of fellow drinkers. The drinking stories we would tell each other caused huge amusement and served as the endorsement of our own lifestyle. We were jolly fellows who enjoyed life. Others were boring, unfulfilled and deserved our pity.

Let's face it; a lot of us were mentally ill.

It takes really serious illness almost to the point of fatality; great and irreconcilable personal loss; or death itself to bring an end to this cycle.

I was lucky that my wife and daughter walked out when they did. The loss was great and in my case irreconcilable enough. I was lucky that my daughter Tara came to see me when she did to talk me down for three days and face my completely unreasonable anger, whilst she set about getting me to visit a doctor. I was lucky that the doctor was persuasive enough to get me to see the psychiatrist. I was lucky that my insurance could pay for my stay at The Priory. I was lucky that I had a thoroughly unpleasant bully of a counsellor who did not give up on me. Despite himself, he was what I needed. I was lucky that I persisted with AA meetings. I was lucky that my good friends stood by me and supported what I was trying to do. I was lucky that my son James found me after nearly forty years. But I was most fortunate when Roseanne and Pia, Tara and Petra came back into my life.

I never set out then or now to tell other people how to help themselves in this sort of situation, but it would be selfish not to share some of the things I believe that I have learned.

Undoubtedly, genetics must have something to do with addiction, but that explanation can be blurred with family history and background. It's the old nature versus nurture argument. There is a saying in AA that if you removed all the Scots and Irish you could hold AA meetings in a telephone box.

Emotional trauma at an impressionable age must certainly be a contributing factor. Yet the counter argument to be put forward is that many people have emotional traumas in their childhood and teens and do not suffer from addictive behaviour in later life.

Being weak-minded or lacking self-discipline is what a lot of worthy people might say. Sure, that's true but there are many strong minded and disciplined people who can behave addictively as well. The incidence of alcoholism amongst the 'caring' professions, such as medicine, is seven times the average incidence of alcoholism.

Every human being is as unique as a snowflake. They say that one in five adults in the 'western world' shows signs of addictive behaviour. It can express itself through alcohol or drugs, sex or shoplifting, gambling or anorexia, obsessive-compulsive behaviour or over-work. It's part of the modern, human condition. The incidence of addictive behaviour has probably been around for as long. Vastly improved productivity, instant and conceivably de-humanising communication obtained by social media and the World Wide Web, too much leisure time and the erosion of self-discipline as a key tenet of organised religion and its diminution, has contributed vastly to it and may even be causing the growth of addictive behaviour.

They are only my theories though, and I am absolutely in no position to tell someone else how to regain control of their lives. I can only say that true self-awareness has to be a vital ingredient. Self-awareness not self-centeredness is the key. Only at the later stages comes the issue about the chemical properties of alcohol. It is much more about recognising and overcoming the underlying psychosis. One of the definitions of psychosis includes the phrase 'delusional' and 'lack of insight and self-awareness'.

I now ask myself why I always needed to be the last man standing. Why did I have to think so little of myself that I had to drink to be able to communicate and be liked? Isn't it curious that alcoholics often hang on to their jobs even though they may lose their wives, families, houses and friends? It is quite easy to work out when you think of it. They cannot pay for drink if they lose their jobs!

In the face of being liked and loved by my parents, by my siblings and by my own partners and children, why did I not trust and draw confidence from that? Why did I keep travelling just for the sake of travelling? Why didn't I stop and deal with things and face them?

Restlessness and boredom suggest themselves as causes, but I led an interesting and, on occasions, even a fulfilling life. I just never stopped and factored in self-awareness.

There is very little that I regret now. I'm alive and relatively healthy whilst weighing two stone less than before, but probably still two stone too much. I have had a fantastically varied life. I have seen a significant part of this planet. I have met hundreds of interesting people. I've not made very much money, but I have enough. I have loving, intelligent, well-educated and healthy children who now know me for what I am.

It could even be said that I am now beginning to know me for what I am.

I have a forgiving friend in my first wife. I have offspring who tolerate me with great good humour. I have an extraordinarily generous, intelligent and good-humoured second wife of forty-five years who has actually encouraged me to write this book and who very much knows me for what I am.

In fact, that's how I got here from there.

Printed in Great Britain
by Amazon